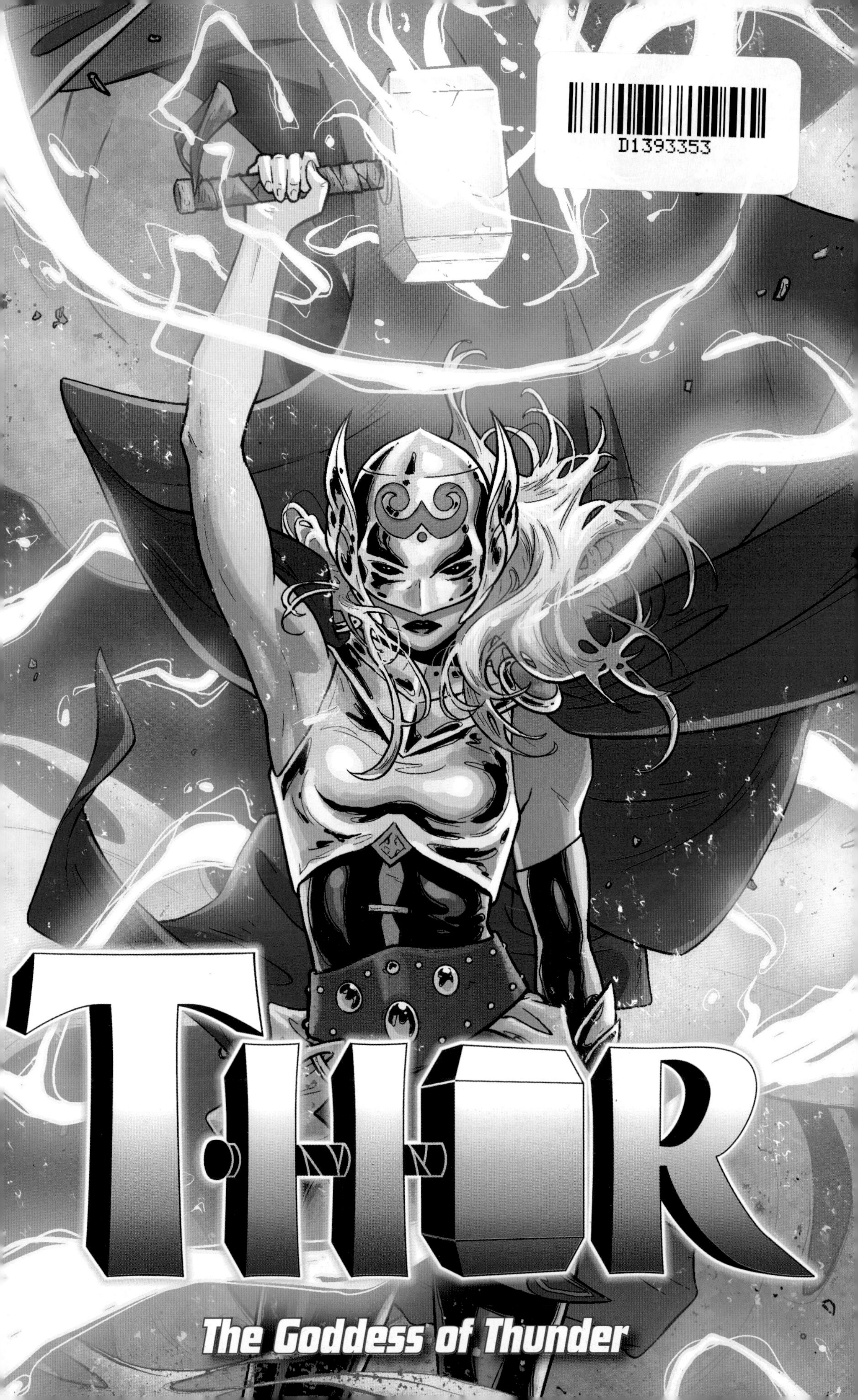

THOR

The Goddess of Thunder

THOR

The Goddess of Thunder

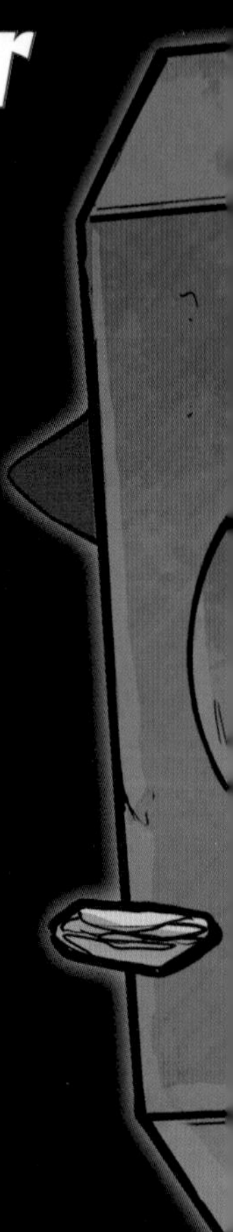

WRITER:
JASON AARON

ARTIST:
RUSSELL DAUTERMAN & JORGE MOLINA

COLOUR ARTIST:
MATTHEW WILSON & JORGE MOLINA

LETTERS:
VIRTUAL CALLIGRAPHY'S JOE SABINO

ASSISTANT EDITOR: JON MOISAN

EDITOR: WILL MOSS

PUBLISHER: DAN BUCKLEY

CHIEF CREATIVE OFFICER: JOE QUESADA

EXECUTIVE PRODUCER: ALAN FINE

EDITOR-IN-CHIEF: AXEL ALONSO

COVER ART: RUSSELL DAUTERMAN & FRANK MARTIN

you have any comments or queries about Thor Vol. 1: The Goddess of Thunder? Email us at graphicnovels@panini.co.uk!

marvel.com

© 2016 Marvel

TM & © 2014, 2015 & 2016 Marvel & Subs. Licensed by Marvel Characters B.V. through Panini S.p.A, Italy. All Rights Reserved. First printing 2015. Third impression 2016. Published by Panini Publishing, a division of Panini UK Limited. Mike Riddell, Managing Director. Alan O'Keefe, Managing Editor. Mark Irvine, Production Manager. Marco M. Lupoi, Publishing Director Europe. Brady Webb, Reprint Editor. Samuel Taylor, Assistant Reprint Editor. Rosanna Stewart, Designer. Office of publication: Brockbourne House, 77 Mount Ephraim, Tunbridge Wells, Kent TN4 8BS. This publication may not be sold, except by authorised dealers, and is sold subject to the condition that it shall not be sold or distributed with any part of its cover or markings removed, nor in a mutilated condition. Printed in Italy by Terrazzi. ISBN: 978-1-84653-656-4.

MARVEL GRAPHIC NOVEL

THOR #1

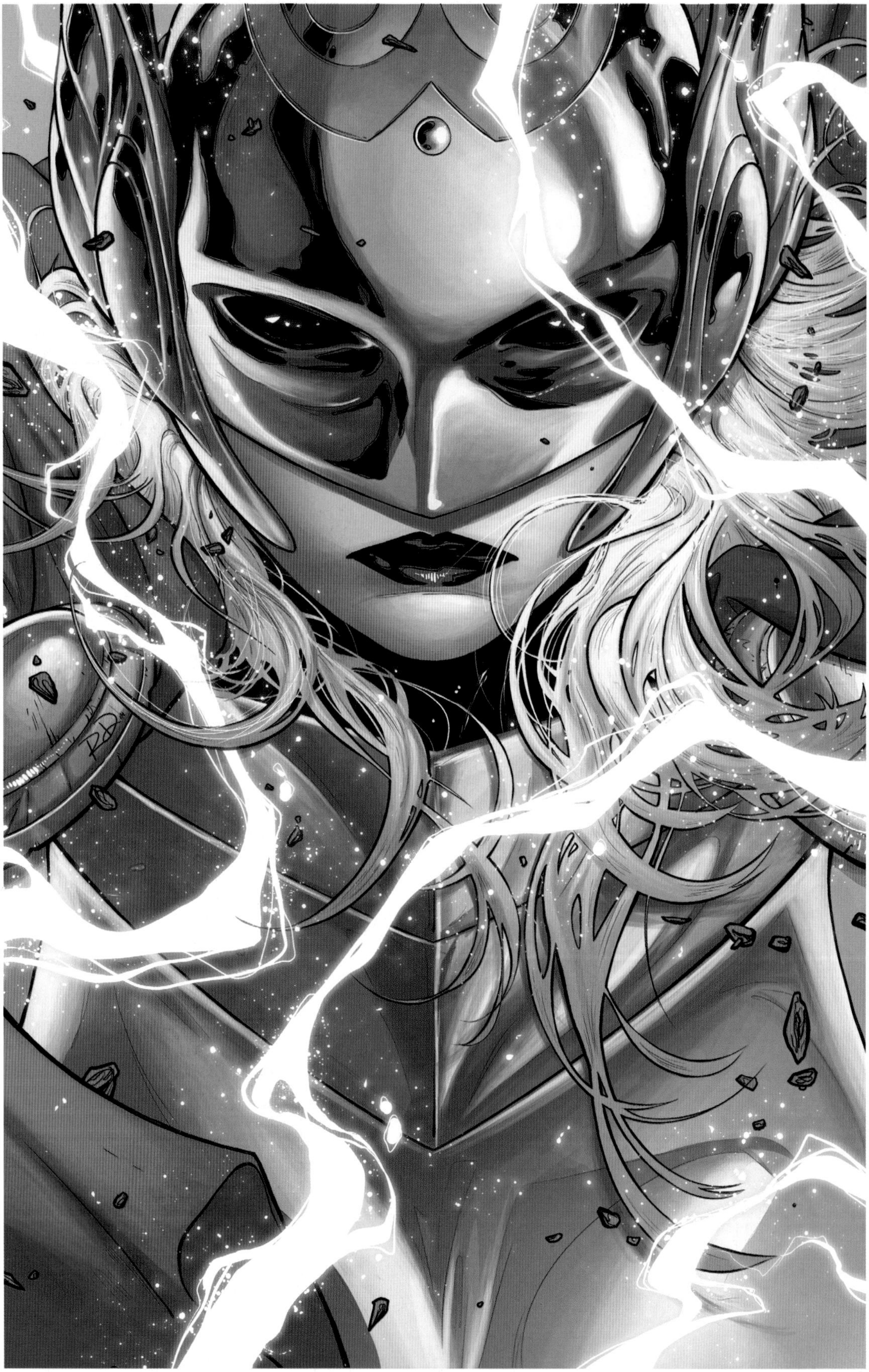

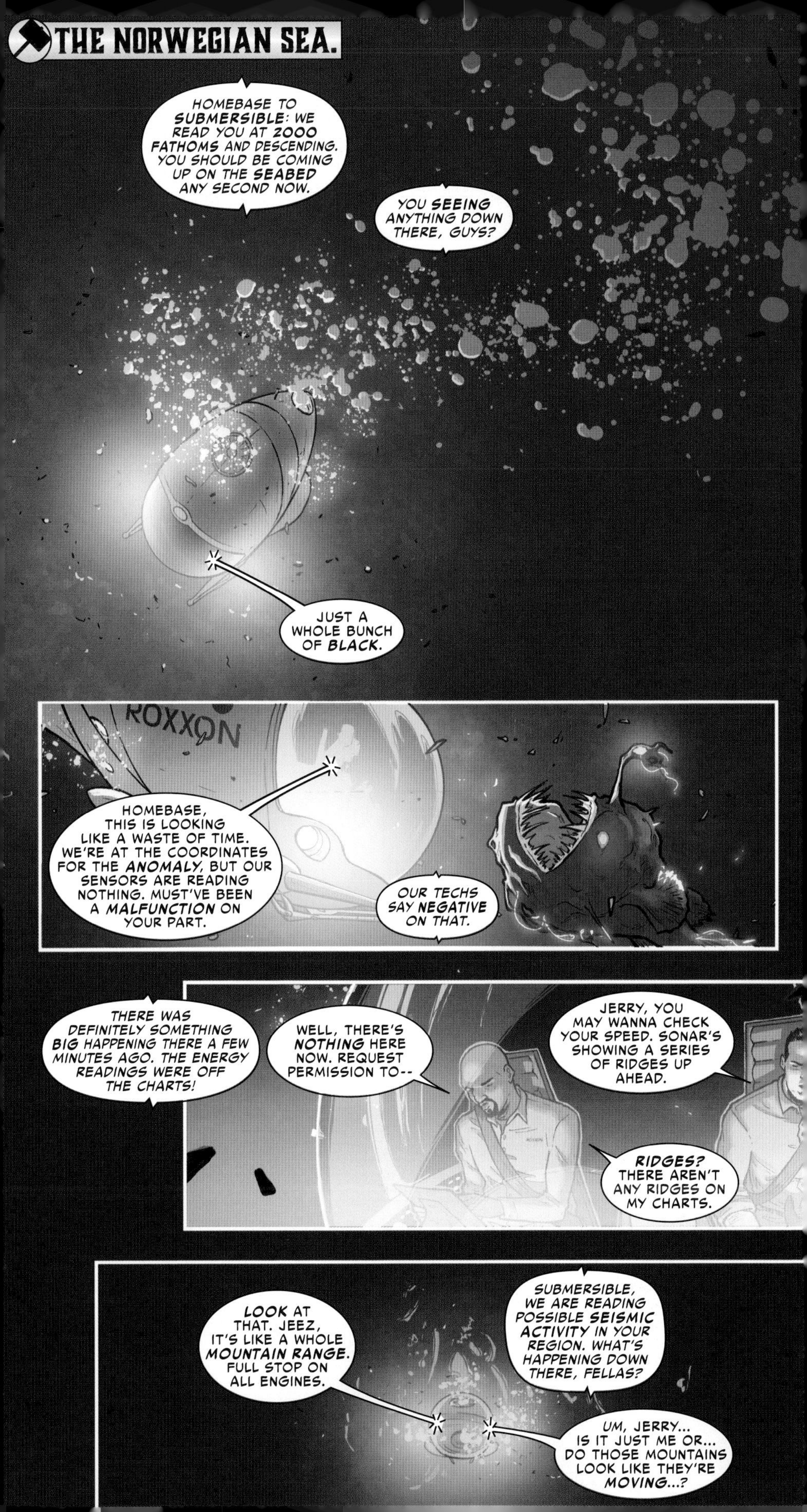
THE NORWEGIAN SEA.
HOMEBASE TO SUBMERSIBLE: WE READ YOU AT 2000 FATHOMS AND DESCENDING. YOU SHOULD BE COMING UP ON THE SEABED ANY SECOND NOW.
YOU SEEING ANYTHING DOWN THERE, GUYS?
JUST A WHOLE BUNCH OF BLACK.
ROXXON
HOMEBASE, THIS IS LOOKING LIKE A WASTE OF TIME. WE'RE AT THE COORDINATES FOR THE ANOMALY, BUT OUR SENSORS ARE READING NOTHING. MUST'VE BEEN A MALFUNCTION ON YOUR PART.
OUR TECHS SAY NEGATIVE ON THAT.
THERE WAS DEFINITELY SOMETHING BIG HAPPENING THERE A FEW MINUTES AGO. THE ENERGY READINGS WERE OFF THE CHARTS!
WELL, THERE'S NOTHING HERE NOW. REQUEST PERMISSION TO--
JERRY, YOU MAY WANNA CHECK YOUR SPEED. SONAR'S SHOWING A SERIES OF RIDGES UP AHEAD.
RIDGES? THERE AREN'T ANY RIDGES ON MY CHARTS.
LOOK AT THAT. JEEZ, IT'S LIKE A WHOLE MOUNTAIN RANGE. FULL STOP ON ALL ENGINES.
SUBMERSIBLE, WE ARE READING POSSIBLE SEISMIC ACTIVITY IN YOUR REGION. WHAT'S HAPPENING DOWN THERE, FELLAS?
UM, JERRY... IS IT JUST ME OR... DO THOSE MOUNTAINS LOOK LIKE THEY'RE MOVING...?

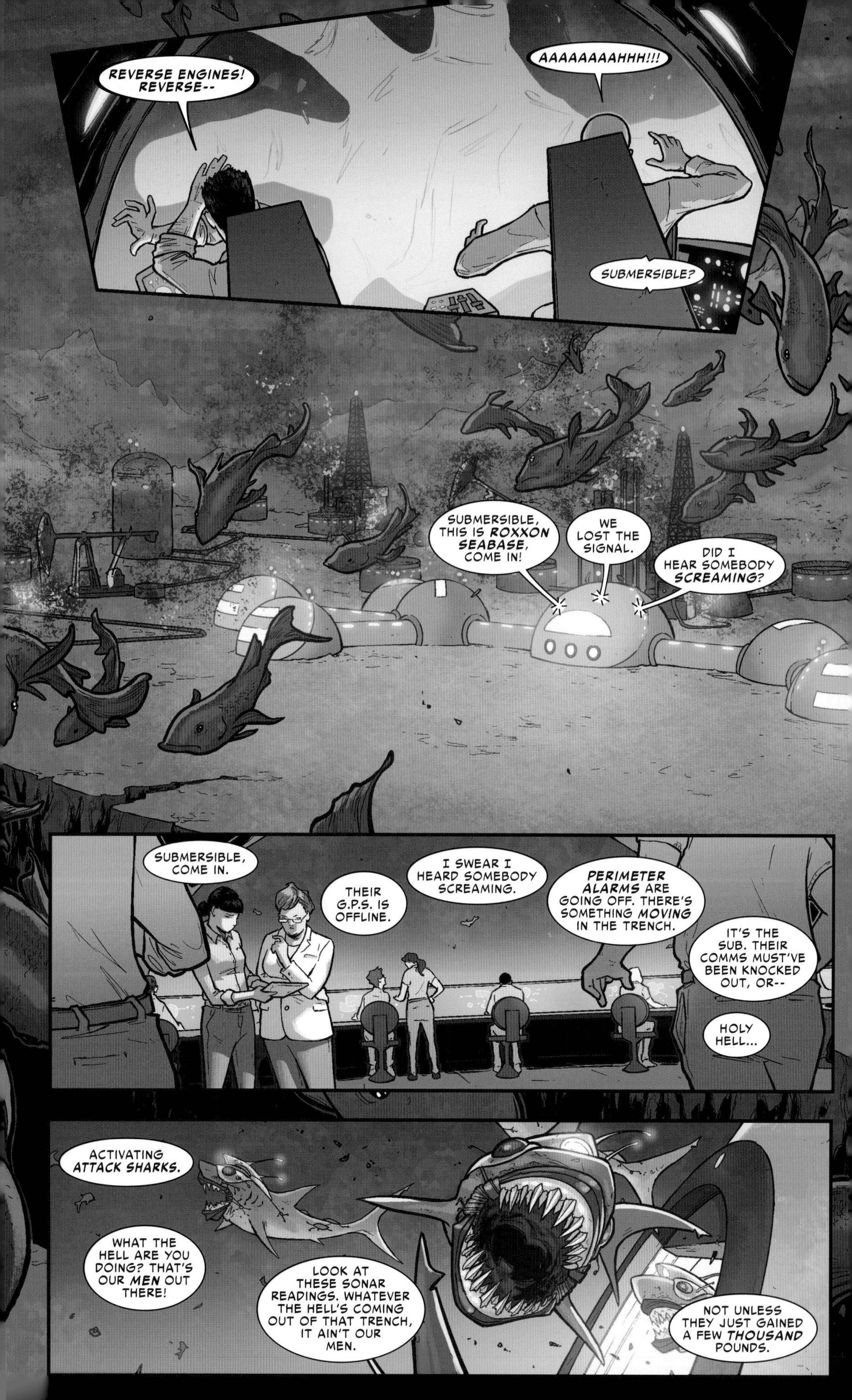
REVERSE ENGINES! REVERSE--
AAAAAAAAHHH!!!
SUBMERSIBLE?
SUBMERSIBLE, THIS IS ROXXON SEABASE, COME IN!
WE LOST THE SIGNAL.
DID I HEAR SOMEBODY SCREAMING?
SUBMERSIBLE, COME IN.
THEIR G.P.S. IS OFFLINE.
I SWEAR I HEARD SOMEBODY SCREAMING.
PERIMETER ALARMS ARE GOING OFF. THERE'S SOMETHING MOVING IN THE TRENCH.
IT'S THE SUB. THEIR COMMS MUST'VE BEEN KNOCKED OUT, OR--
HOLY HELL...
ACTIVATING ATTACK SHARKS.
WHAT THE HELL ARE YOU DOING? THAT'S OUR MEN OUT THERE!
LOOK AT THESE SONAR READINGS. WHATEVER THE HELL'S COMING OUT OF THAT TRENCH, IT AIN'T OUR MEN.
NOT UNLESS THEY JUST GAINED A FEW THOUSAND POUNDS.

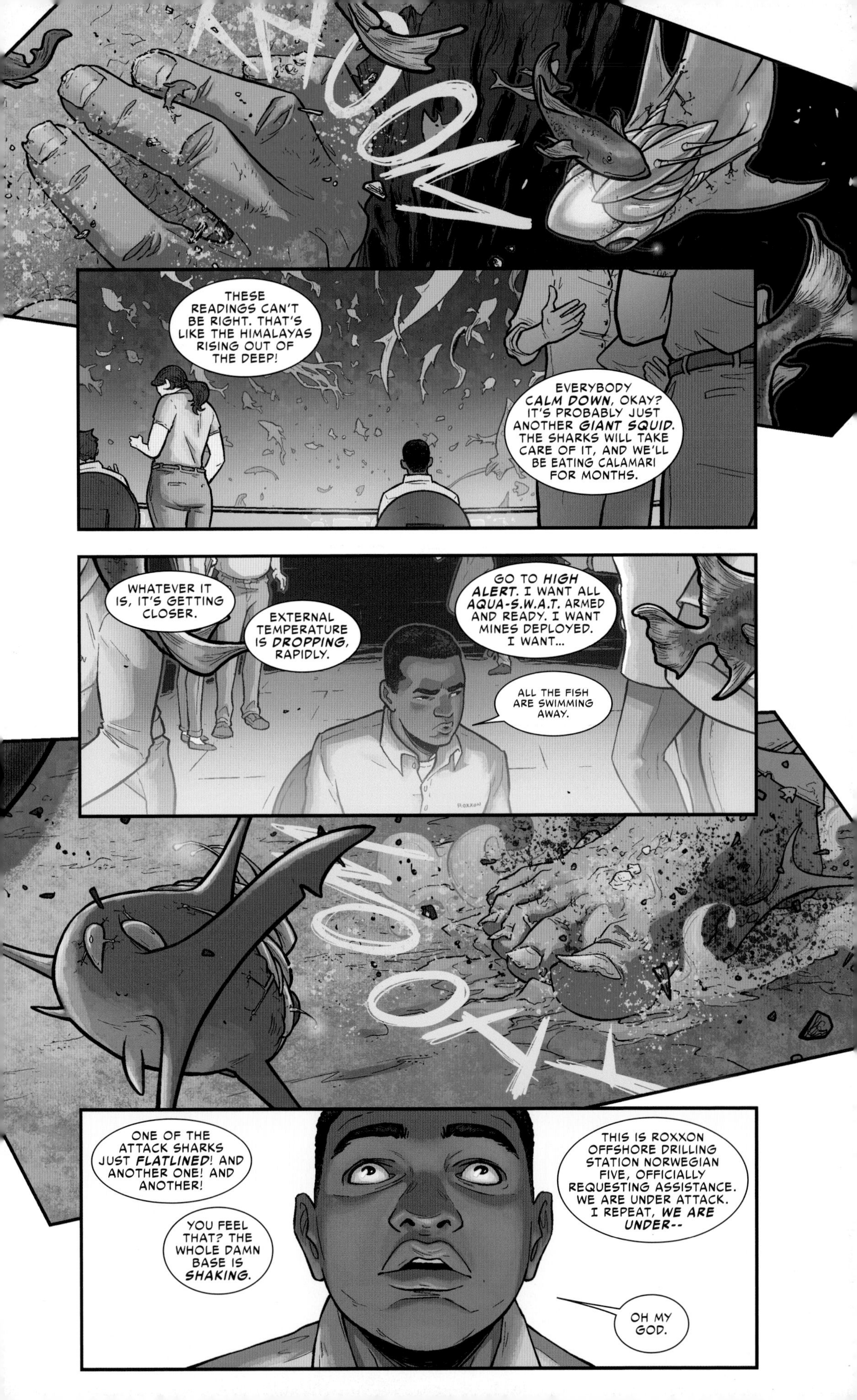
THESE READINGS CAN'T BE RIGHT. THAT'S LIKE THE HIMALAYAS RISING OUT OF THE DEEP!
EVERYBODY CALM DOWN, OKAY? IT'S PROBABLY JUST ANOTHER GIANT SQUID. THE SHARKS WILL TAKE CARE OF IT, AND WE'LL BE EATING CALAMARI FOR MONTHS.
WHATEVER IT IS, IT'S GETTING CLOSER.
EXTERNAL TEMPERATURE IS DROPPING, RAPIDLY.
GO TO HIGH ALERT. I WANT ALL AQUA-S.W.A.T. ARMED AND READY. I WANT MINES DEPLOYED. I WANT...
ALL THE FISH ARE SWIMMING AWAY.
ROXXON
ONE OF THE ATTACK SHARKS JUST FLATLINED! AND ANOTHER ONE! AND ANOTHER!
YOU FEEL THAT? THE WHOLE DAMN BASE IS SHAKING.
THIS IS ROXXON OFFSHORE DRILLING STATION NORWEGIAN FIVE, OFFICIALLY REQUESTING ASSISTANCE. WE ARE UNDER ATTACK. I REPEAT, WE ARE UNDER--
OH MY GOD.

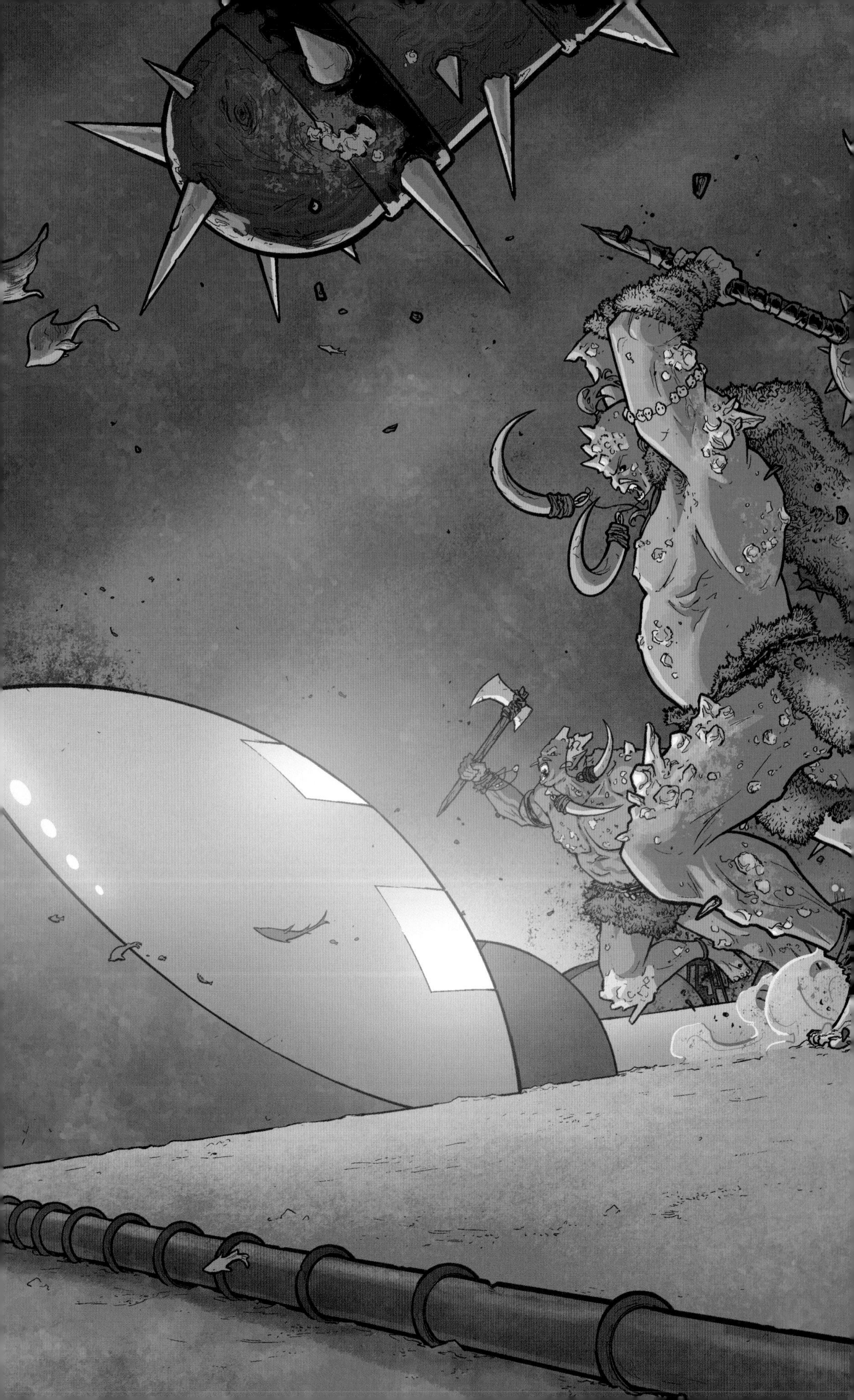

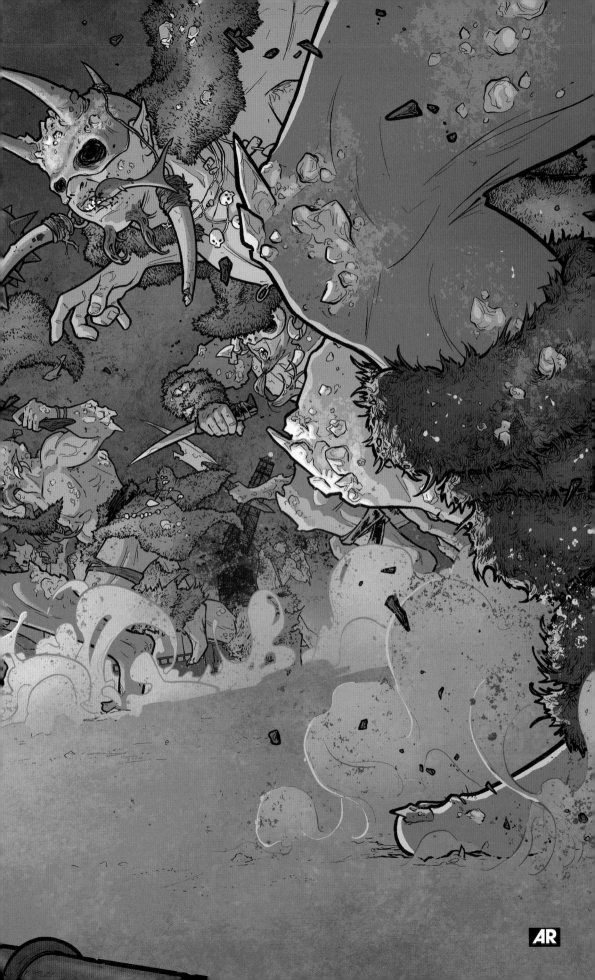

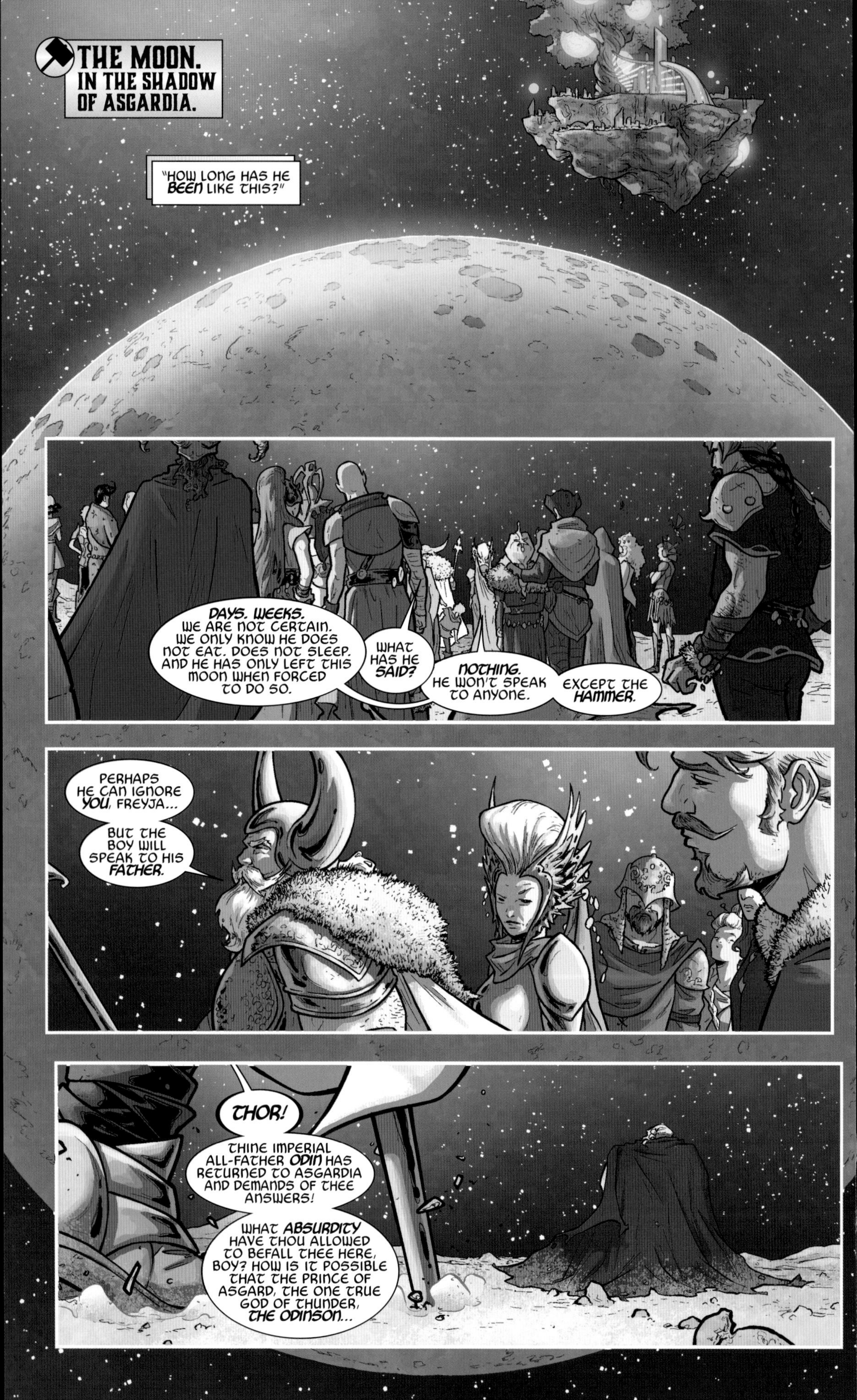
THE MOON. IN THE SHADOW OF ASGARDIA.
"HOW LONG HAS HE BEEN LIKE THIS?"
DAYS. WEEKS. WE ARE NOT CERTAIN. WE ONLY KNOW HE DOES NOT EAT. DOES NOT SLEEP. AND HE HAS ONLY LEFT THIS MOON WHEN FORCED TO DO SO.
WHAT HAS HE SAID?
NOTHING. HE WON'T SPEAK TO ANYONE.
EXCEPT THE HAMMER.
PERHAPS HE CAN IGNORE YOU, FREYJA...
BUT THE BOY WILL SPEAK TO HIS FATHER.
THOR!
THINE IMPERIAL ALL-FATHER ODIN HAS RETURNED TO ASGARDIA AND DEMANDS OF THEE ANSWERS!
WHAT ABSURDITY HAVE THOU ALLOWED TO BEFALL THEE HERE, BOY? HOW IS IT POSSIBLE THAT THE PRINCE OF ASGARD, THE ONE TRUE GOD OF THUNDER, THE ODINSON...

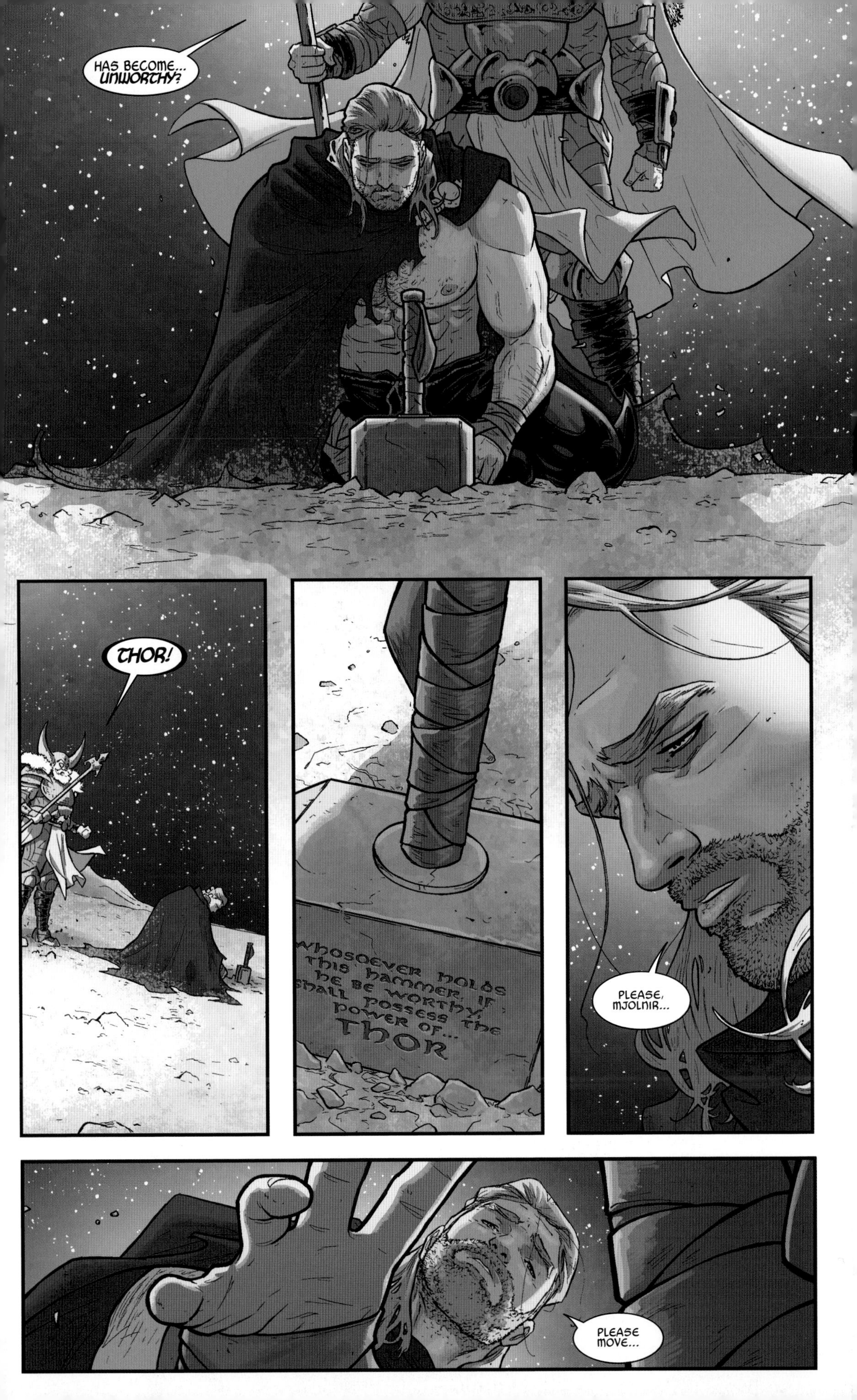
HAS BECOME... UNWORTHY?
THOR!
WHOSOEVER HOLDS THIS HAMMER, IF HE BE WORTHY, SHALL POSSESS THE POWER OF... THOR
PLEASE, MJOLNIR...
PLEASE MOVE...

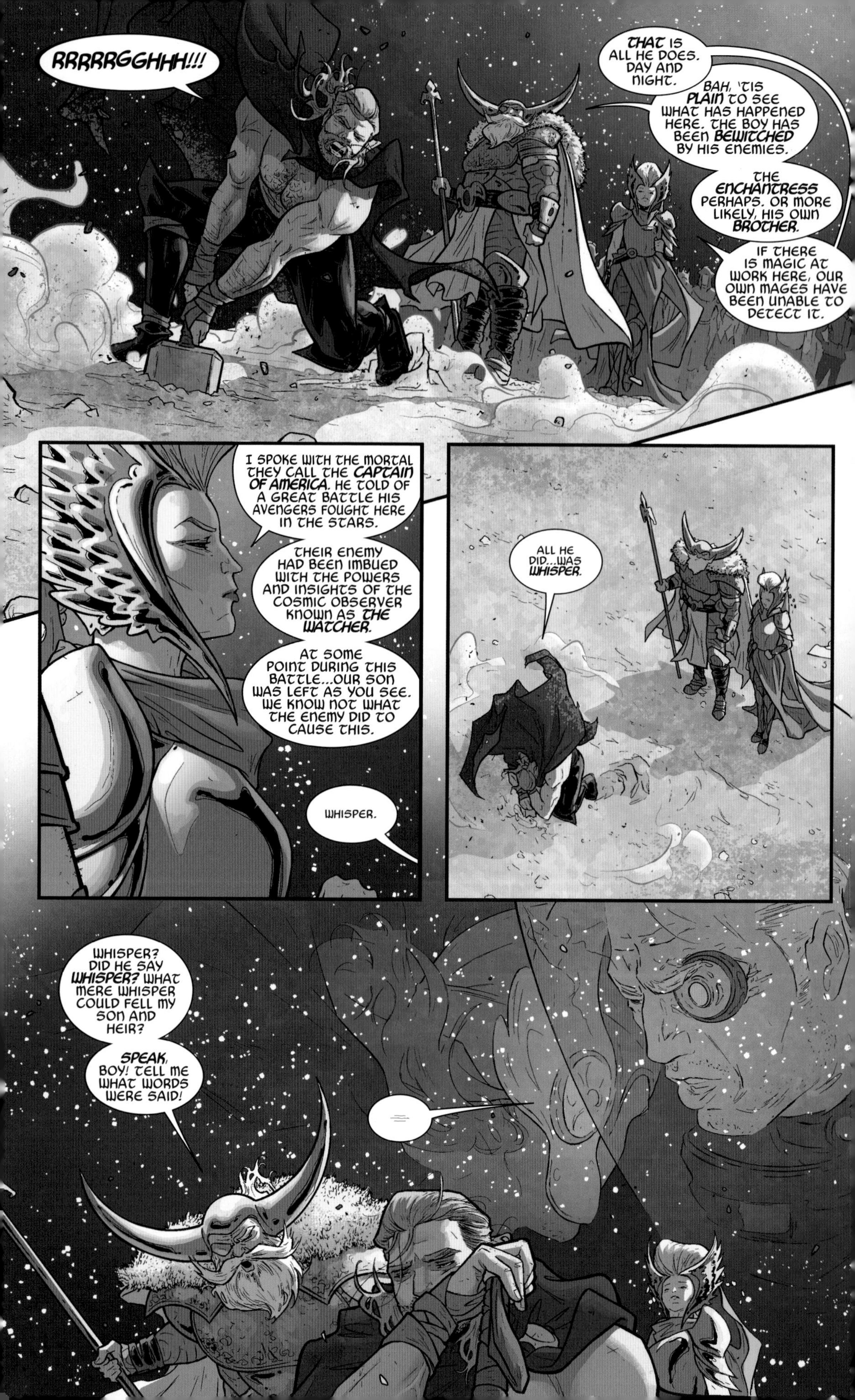
RRRRRGGHHH!!!
THAT IS ALL HE DOES. DAY AND NIGHT.
BAH, 'TIS PLAIN TO SEE WHAT HAS HAPPENED HERE. THE BOY HAS BEEN BEWITCHED BY HIS ENEMIES.
THE ENCHANTRESS PERHAPS. OR MORE LIKELY, HIS OWN BROTHER.
IF THERE IS MAGIC AT WORK HERE, OUR OWN MAGES HAVE BEEN UNABLE TO DETECT IT.
I SPOKE WITH THE MORTAL THEY CALL THE CAPTAIN OF AMERICA. HE TOLD OF A GREAT BATTLE HIS AVENGERS FOUGHT HERE IN THE STARS.
THEIR ENEMY HAD BEEN IMBUED WITH THE POWERS AND INSIGHTS OF THE COSMIC OBSERVER KNOWN AS THE WATCHER.
AT SOME POINT DURING THIS BATTLE...OUR SON WAS LEFT AS YOU SEE. WE KNOW NOT WHAT THE ENEMY DID TO CAUSE THIS.
WHISPER.
ALL HE DID...WAS WHISPER.
WHISPER? DID HE SAY WHISPER? WHAT MERE WHISPER COULD FELL MY SON AND HEIR?
SPEAK, BOY! TELL ME WHAT WORDS WERE SAID!

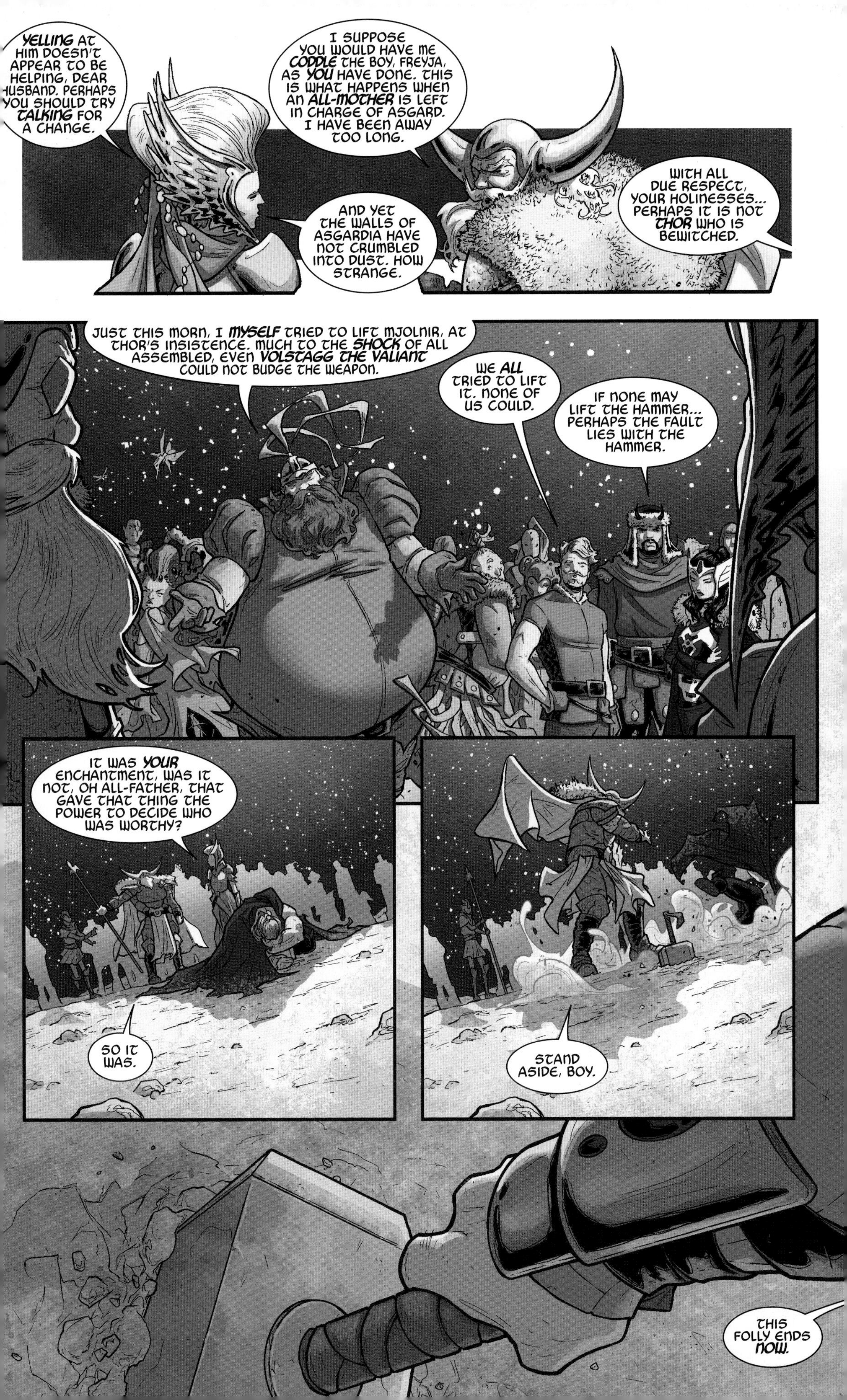
YELLING AT HIM DOESN'T APPEAR TO BE HELPING, DEAR HUSBAND. PERHAPS YOU SHOULD TRY TALKING FOR A CHANGE.
I SUPPOSE YOU WOULD HAVE ME CODDLE THE BOY, FREYJA, AS YOU HAVE DONE. THIS IS WHAT HAPPENS WHEN AN ALL-MOTHER IS LEFT IN CHARGE OF ASGARD. I HAVE BEEN AWAY TOO LONG.
AND YET THE WALLS OF ASGARDIA HAVE NOT CRUMBLED INTO DUST. HOW STRANGE.
WITH ALL DUE RESPECT, YOUR HOLINESSES... PERHAPS IT IS NOT THOR WHO IS BEWITCHED.
JUST THIS MORN, I MYSELF TRIED TO LIFT MJOLNIR, AT THOR'S INSISTENCE. MUCH TO THE SHOCK OF ALL ASSEMBLED, EVEN VOLSTAGG THE VALIANT COULD NOT BUDGE THE WEAPON.
WE ALL TRIED TO LIFT IT. NONE OF US COULD.
IF NONE MAY LIFT THE HAMMER... PERHAPS THE FAULT LIES WITH THE HAMMER.
IT WAS YOUR ENCHANTMENT, WAS IT NOT, OH ALL-FATHER, THAT GAVE THAT THING THE POWER TO DECIDE WHO WAS WORTHY?
SO IT WAS.
STAND ASIDE, BOY.
THIS FOLLY ENDS NOW.

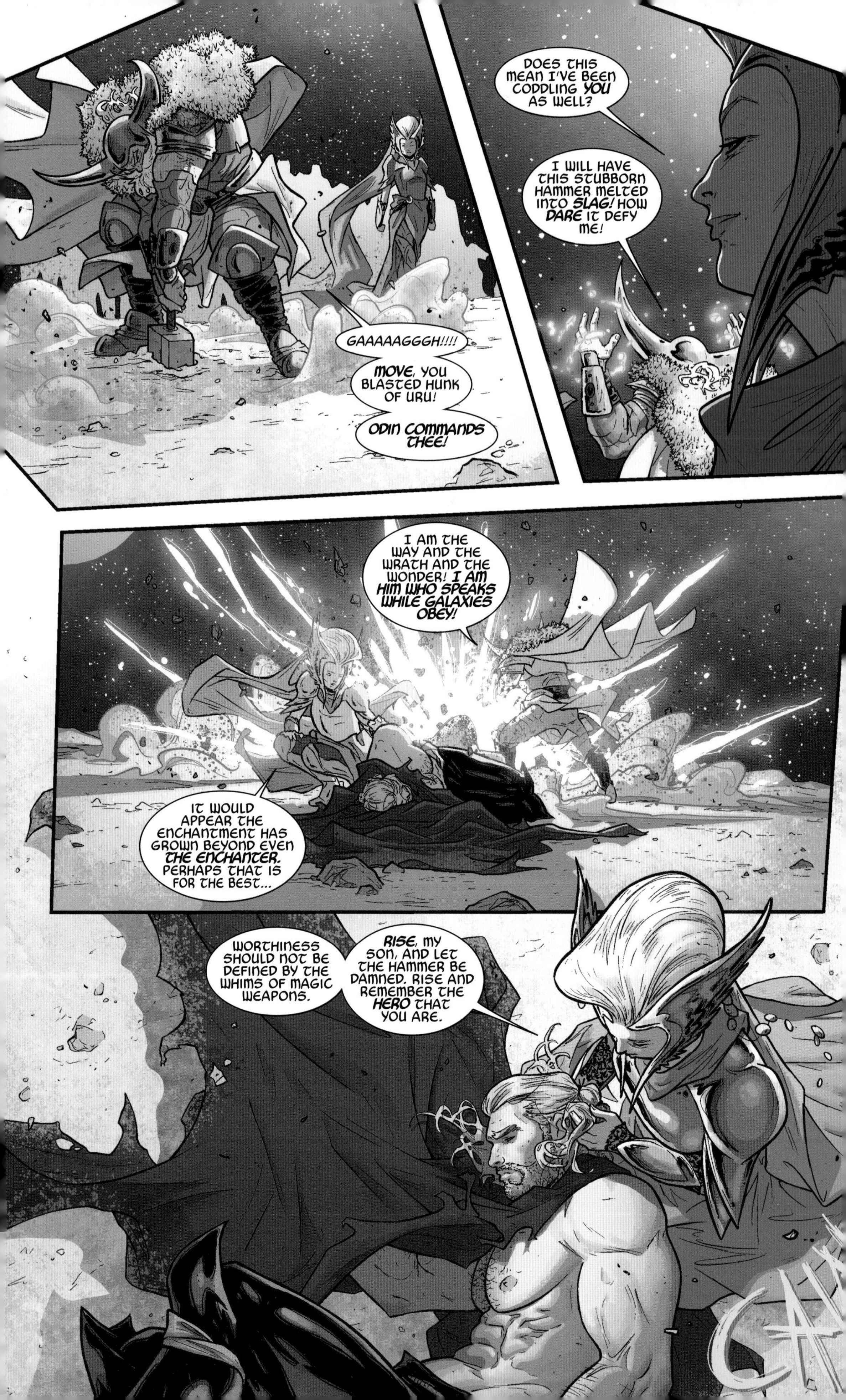

GAAAAAGGGH!!!!
MOVE, YOU BLASTED HUNK OF URU!
ODIN COMMANDS THEE!
DOES THIS MEAN I'VE BEEN CODDLING YOU AS WELL?
I WILL HAVE THIS STUBBORN HAMMER MELTED INTO SLAG! HOW DARE IT DEFY ME!
I AM THE WAY AND THE WRATH AND THE WONDER! I AM HIM WHO SPEAKS WHILE GALAXIES OBEY!
IT WOULD APPEAR THE ENCHANTMENT HAS GROWN BEYOND EVEN THE ENCHANTER. PERHAPS THAT IS FOR THE BEST...
WORTHINESS SHOULD NOT BE DEFINED BY THE WHIMS OF MAGIC WEAPONS.
RISE, MY SON, AND LET THE HAMMER BE DAMNED. RISE AND REMEMBER THE HERO THAT YOU ARE.

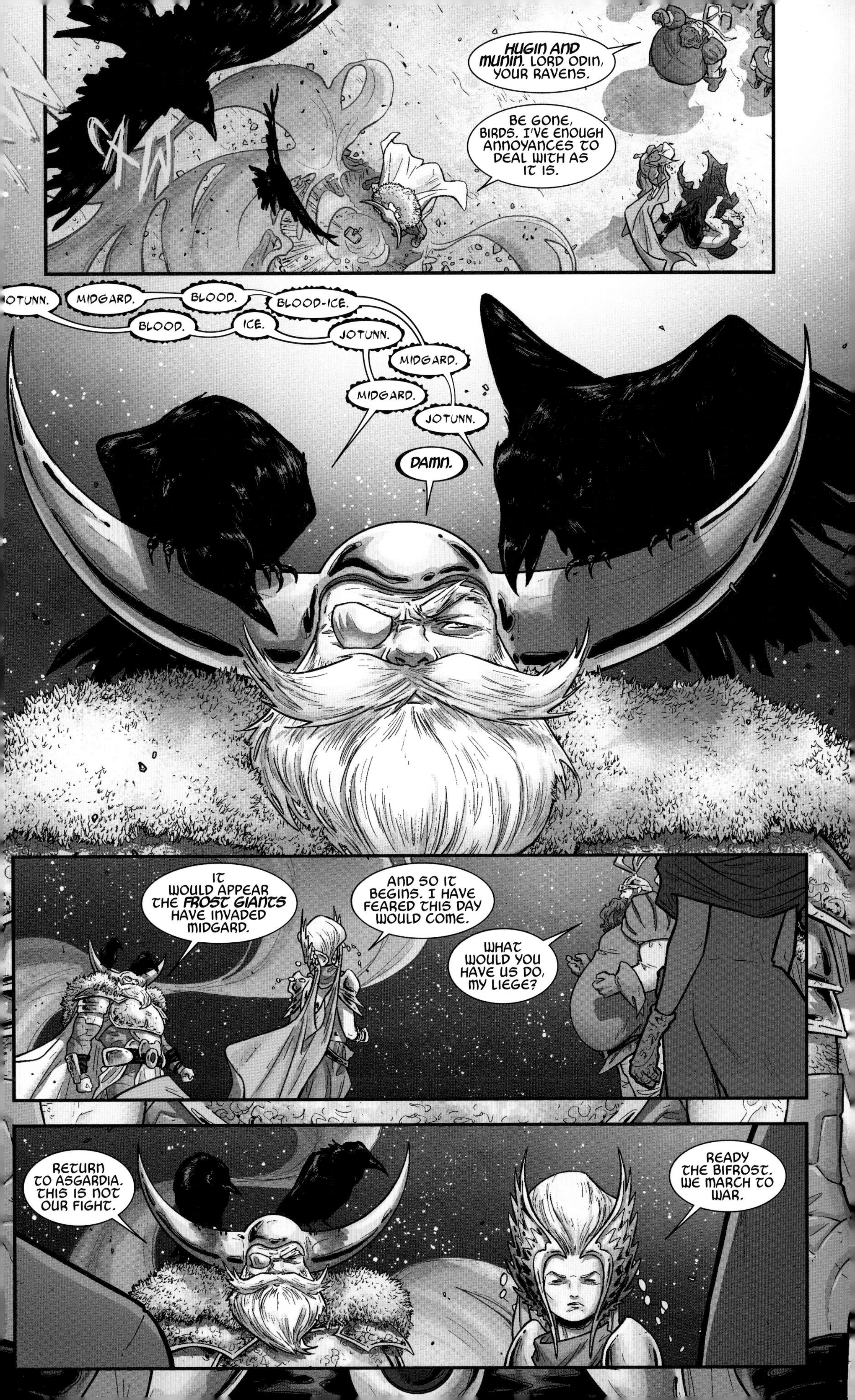
HUGIN AND MUNIN. LORD ODIN, YOUR RAVENS.
BE GONE, BIRDS. I'VE ENOUGH ANNOYANCES TO DEAL WITH AS IT IS.
CAW
JOTUNN.
MIDGARD.
BLOOD.
BLOOD-ICE.
BLOOD.
ICE.
JOTUNN.
MIDGARD.
MIDGARD.
JOTUNN.
DAMN.
IT WOULD APPEAR THE FROST GIANTS HAVE INVADED MIDGARD.
AND SO IT BEGINS. I HAVE FEARED THIS DAY WOULD COME.
WHAT WOULD YOU HAVE US DO, MY LIEGE?
RETURN TO ASGARDIA. THIS IS NOT OUR FIGHT.
READY THE BIFROST. WE MARCH TO WAR.

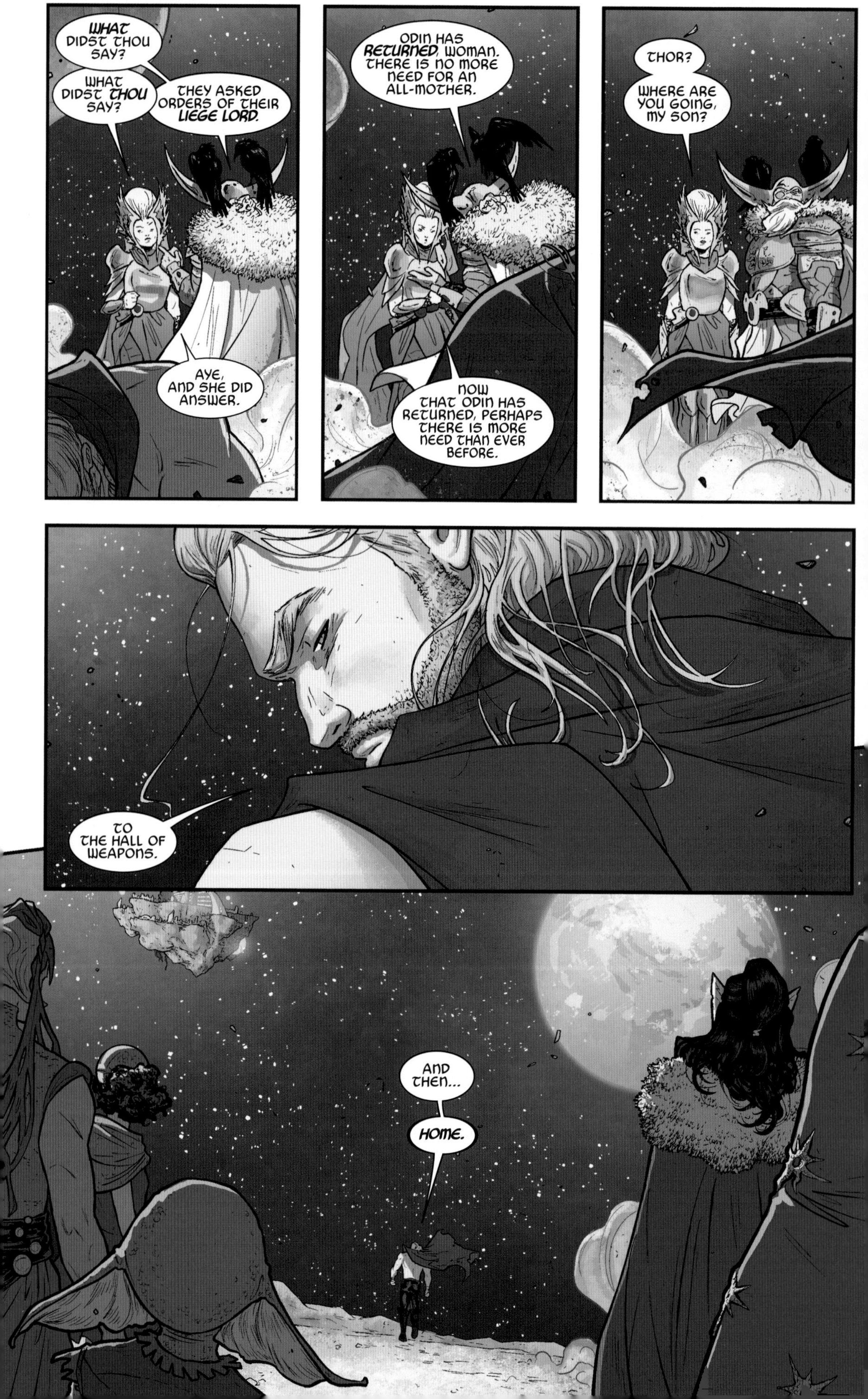
WHAT DIDST THOU SAY?
WHAT DIDST THOU SAY?
THEY ASKED ORDERS OF THEIR LIEGE LORD.
AYE, AND SHE DID ANSWER.
ODIN HAS RETURNED, WOMAN. THERE IS NO MORE NEED FOR AN ALL-MOTHER.
NOW THAT ODIN HAS RETURNED, PERHAPS THERE IS MORE NEED THAN EVER BEFORE.
THOR?
WHERE ARE YOU GOING, MY SON?
TO THE HALL OF WEAPONS.
AND THEN...
HOME.

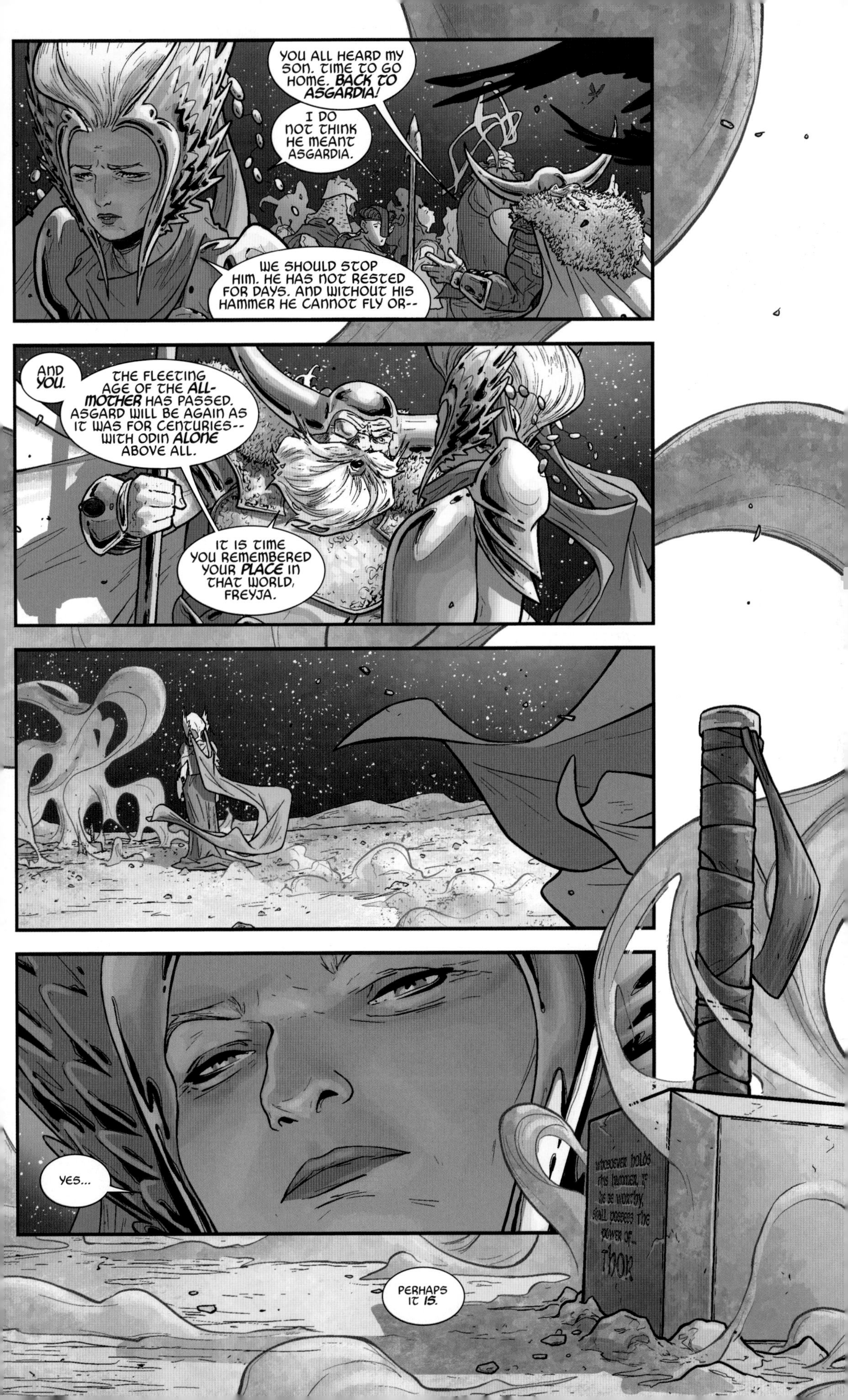
YOU ALL HEARD MY SON. TIME TO GO HOME. BACK TO ASGARDIA!
I DO NOT THINK HE MEANT ASGARDIA.
WE SHOULD STOP HIM. HE HAS NOT RESTED FOR DAYS. AND WITHOUT HIS HAMMER HE CANNOT FLY OR--
AND YOU.
THE FLEETING AGE OF THE ALL-MOTHER HAS PASSED. ASGARD WILL BE AGAIN AS IT WAS FOR CENTURIES-- WITH ODIN ALONE ABOVE ALL.
IT IS TIME YOU REMEMBERED YOUR PLACE IN THAT WORLD, FREYJA.
YES...
WHOSOEVER HOLDS THIS HAMMER, IF HE BE WORTHY, SHALL POSSESS THE POWER OF... THOR
PERHAPS IT IS.

I'VE SEEN THOSE DIVE-TEAMS CUT THROUGH *ATLANTEANS* LIKE THEY WERE DOLPHINS. AND THOSE GIANTS JUST... *SWATTED* THEM AWAY.

ALL DEFENSES ARE DOWN. ALL SUBS DISABLED. COMMS OFFLINE. EVERYTHING THAT ISN'T BROKEN IS *FROZEN*.

GIANTS. I STILL CAN'T BELIEVE IT! WHERE DO THINGS LIKE THAT EVEN *COME* FROM?

THE WESTERN MOUNTAINS OF *JOTUNHEIM*.

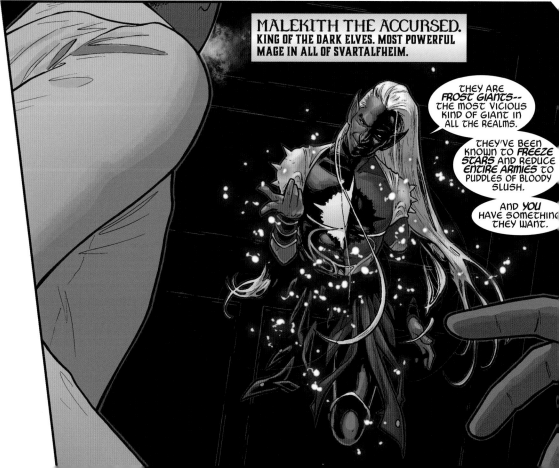

MALEKITH THE ACCURSED. KING OF THE DARK ELVES. MOST POWERFUL MAGE IN ALL OF SVARTALFHEIM.

THEY ARE *FROST GIANTS*-- THE MOST VICIOUS KIND OF GIANT IN ALL THE REALMS.

THEY'VE BEEN KNOWN TO *FREEZE STARS* AND REDUCE *ENTIRE ARMIES* TO PUDDLES OF BLOODY SLUSH.

AND *YOU* HAVE SOMETHING THEY WANT.

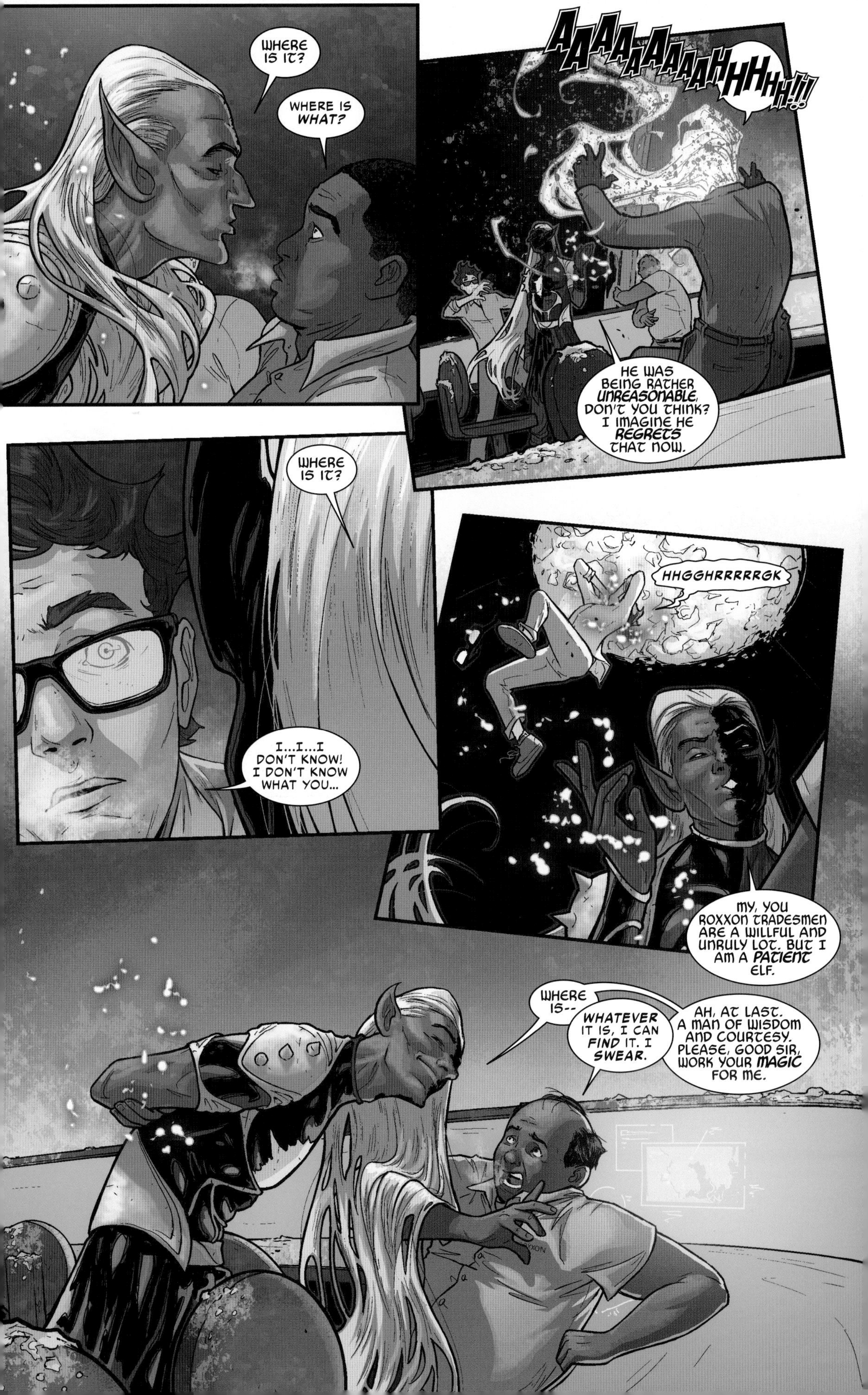
WHERE IS IT?
WHERE IS WHAT?
AAAAAAAAAHHHHH!!!
HE WAS BEING RATHER UNREASONABLE, DON'T YOU THINK? I IMAGINE HE REGRETS THAT NOW.
WHERE IS IT?
I...I...I DON'T KNOW! I DON'T KNOW WHAT YOU...
HHGGHRRRRRGK
MY, YOU ROXXON TRADESMEN ARE A WILLFUL AND UNRULY LOT. BUT I AM A PATIENT ELF.
WHERE IS--
WHATEVER IT IS, I CAN FIND IT. I SWEAR.
AH, AT LAST. A MAN OF WISDOM AND COURTESY. PLEASE, GOOD SIR, WORK YOUR MAGIC FOR ME.

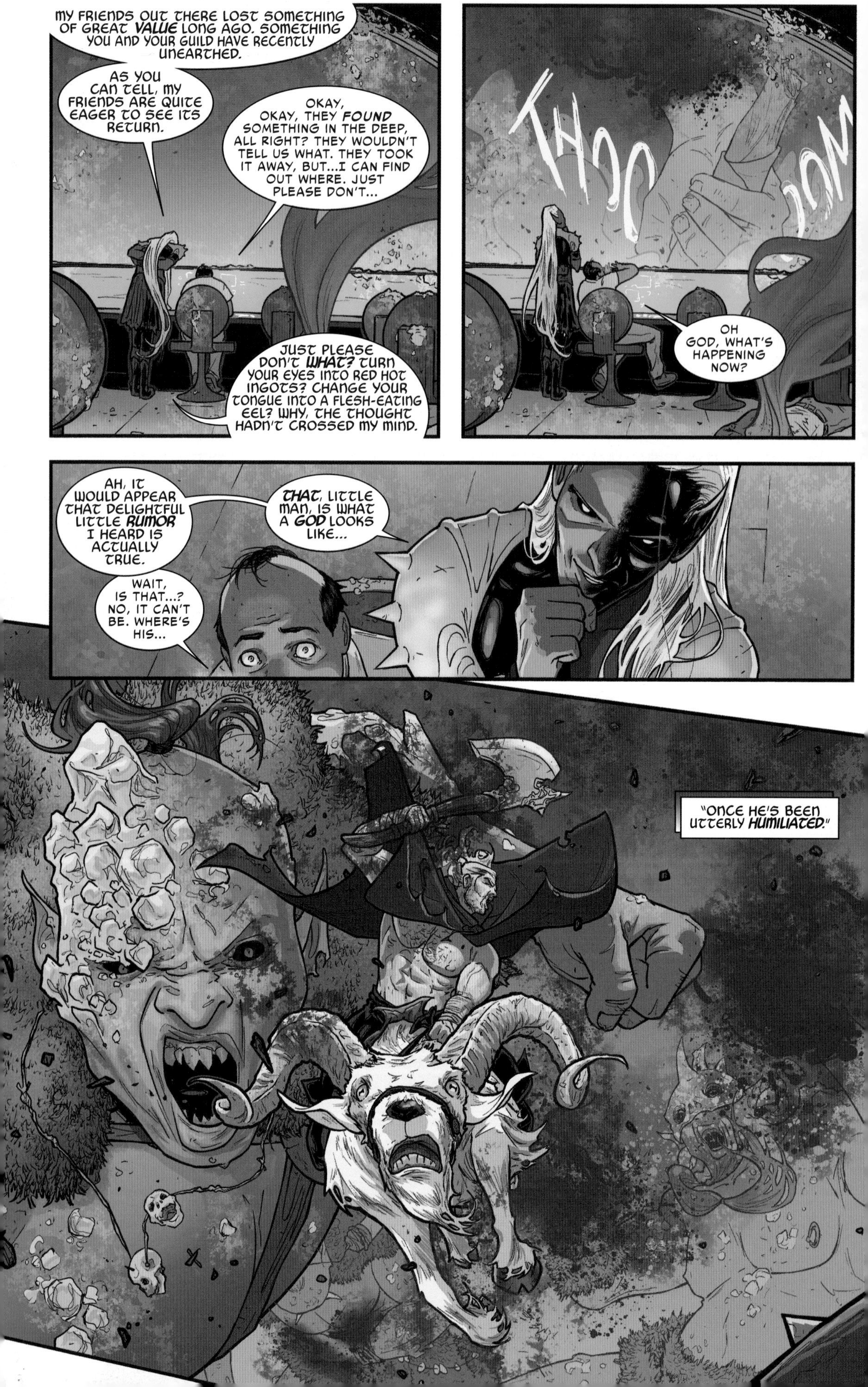

MY FRIENDS OUT THERE LOST SOMETHING OF GREAT VALUE LONG AGO. SOMETHING YOU AND YOUR GUILD HAVE RECENTLY UNEARTHED.
AS YOU CAN TELL, MY FRIENDS ARE QUITE EAGER TO SEE ITS RETURN.
OKAY, OKAY, THEY FOUND SOMETHING IN THE DEEP, ALL RIGHT? THEY WOULDN'T TELL US WHAT. THEY TOOK IT AWAY, BUT...I CAN FIND OUT WHERE. JUST PLEASE DON'T...
JUST PLEASE DON'T WHAT? TURN YOUR EYES INTO RED HOT INGOTS? CHANGE YOUR TONGUE INTO A FLESH-EATING EEL? WHY, THE THOUGHT HADN'T CROSSED MY MIND.
THOOM
OH GOD, WHAT'S HAPPENING NOW?
AH, IT WOULD APPEAR THAT DELIGHTFUL LITTLE RUMOR I HEARD IS ACTUALLY TRUE.
WAIT, IS THAT...? NO, IT CAN'T BE. WHERE'S HIS...
THAT, LITTLE MAN, IS WHAT A GOD LOOKS LIKE...
"ONCE HE'S BEEN UTTERLY HUMILIATED."

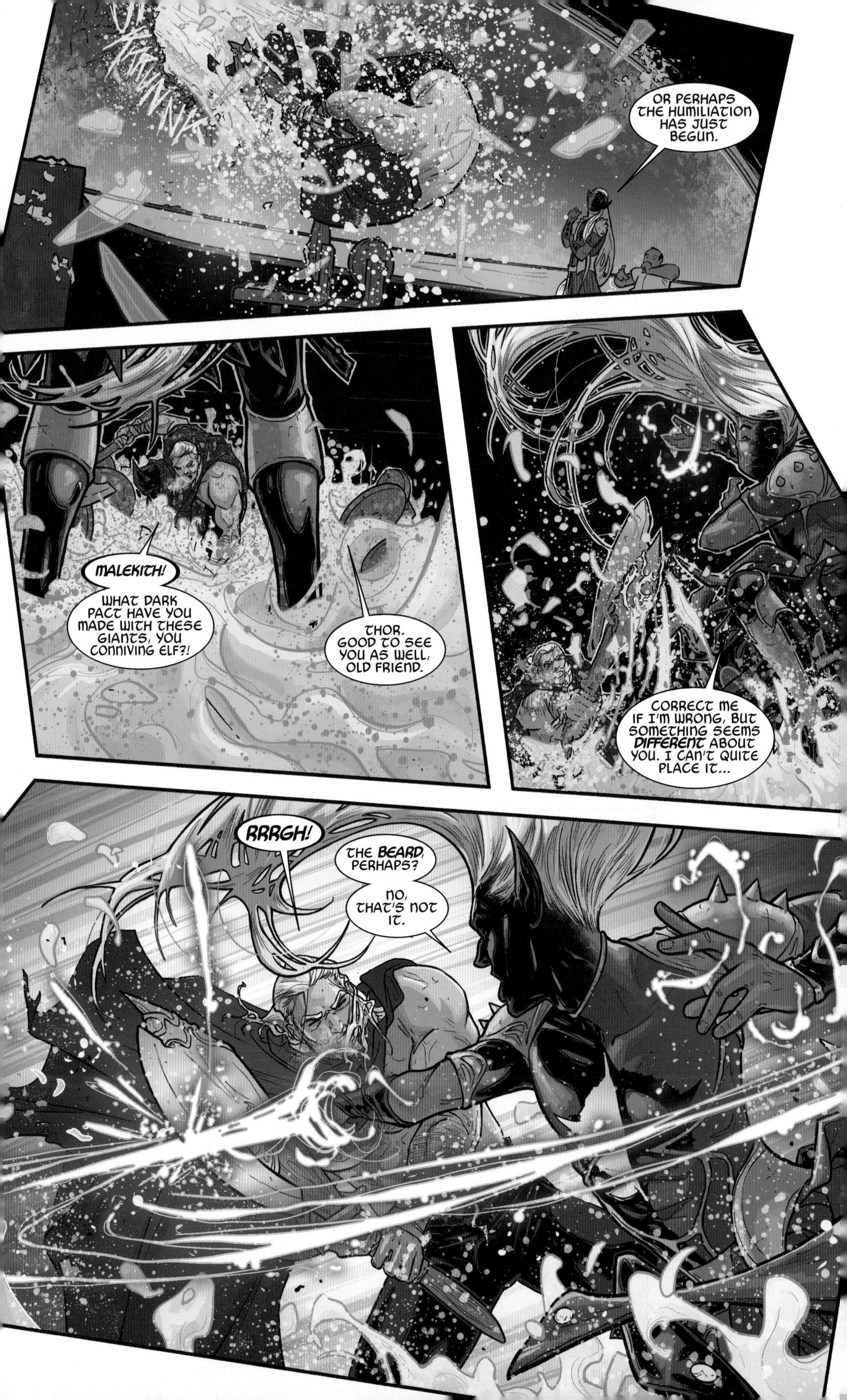
OR PERHAPS THE HUMILIATION HAS JUST BEGUN.
MALEKITH!
WHAT DARK PACT HAVE YOU MADE WITH THESE GIANTS, YOU CONNIVING ELF?!
THOR. GOOD TO SEE YOU AS WELL, OLD FRIEND.
CORRECT ME IF I'M WRONG, BUT SOMETHING SEEMS DIFFERENT ABOUT YOU. I CAN'T QUITE PLACE IT...
RRRGH!
THE BEARD, PERHAPS?
NO, THAT'S NOT IT.

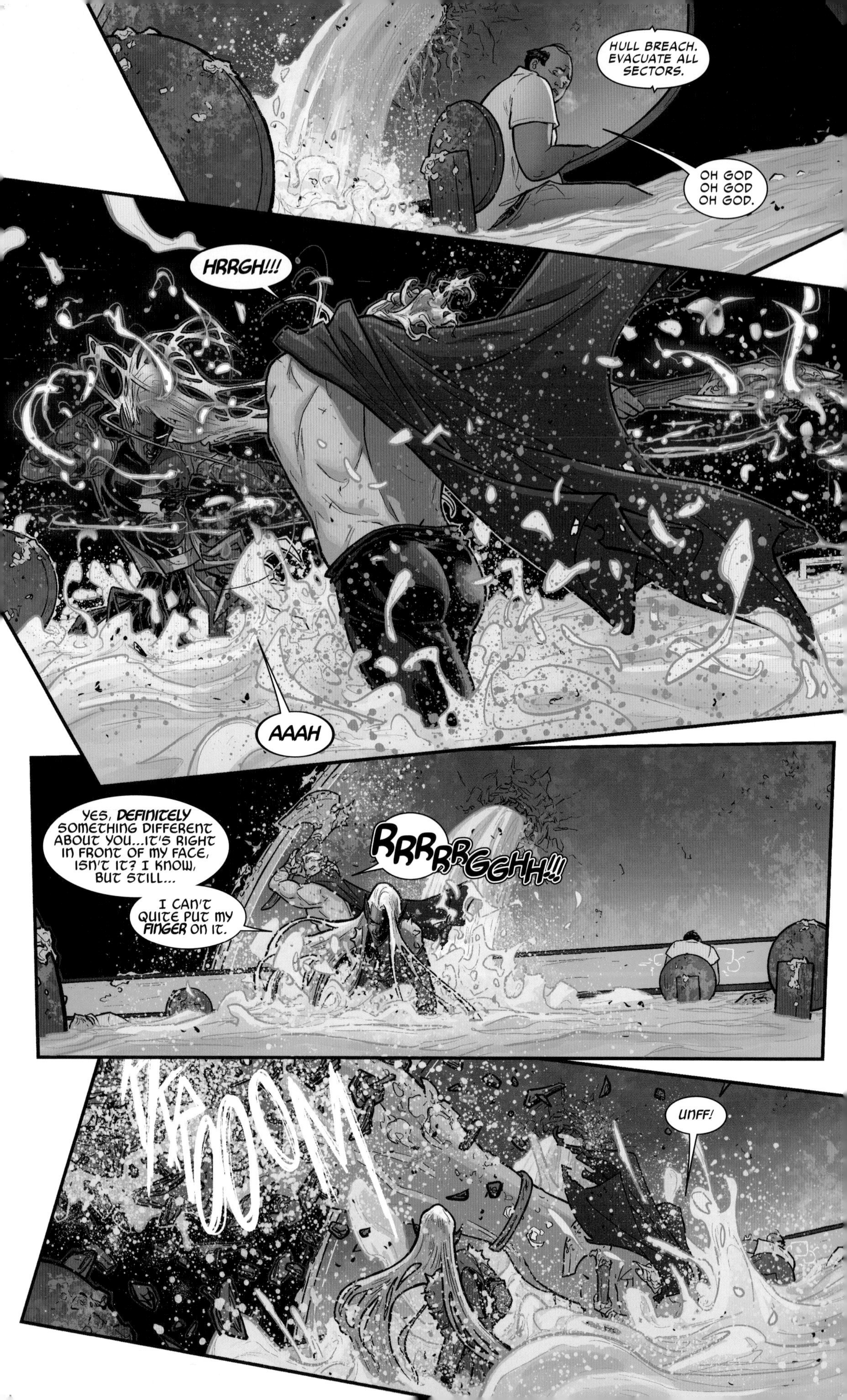
HULL BREACH. EVACUATE ALL SECTORS.
OH GOD OH GOD OH GOD.
HRRGH!!!
AAAH
YES, DEFINITELY SOMETHING DIFFERENT ABOUT YOU...IT'S RIGHT IN FRONT OF MY FACE, ISN'T IT? I KNOW, BUT STILL...
I CAN'T QUITE PUT MY FINGER ON IT.
RRRRRGGHH!!!
KKAOOOM
UNFF!

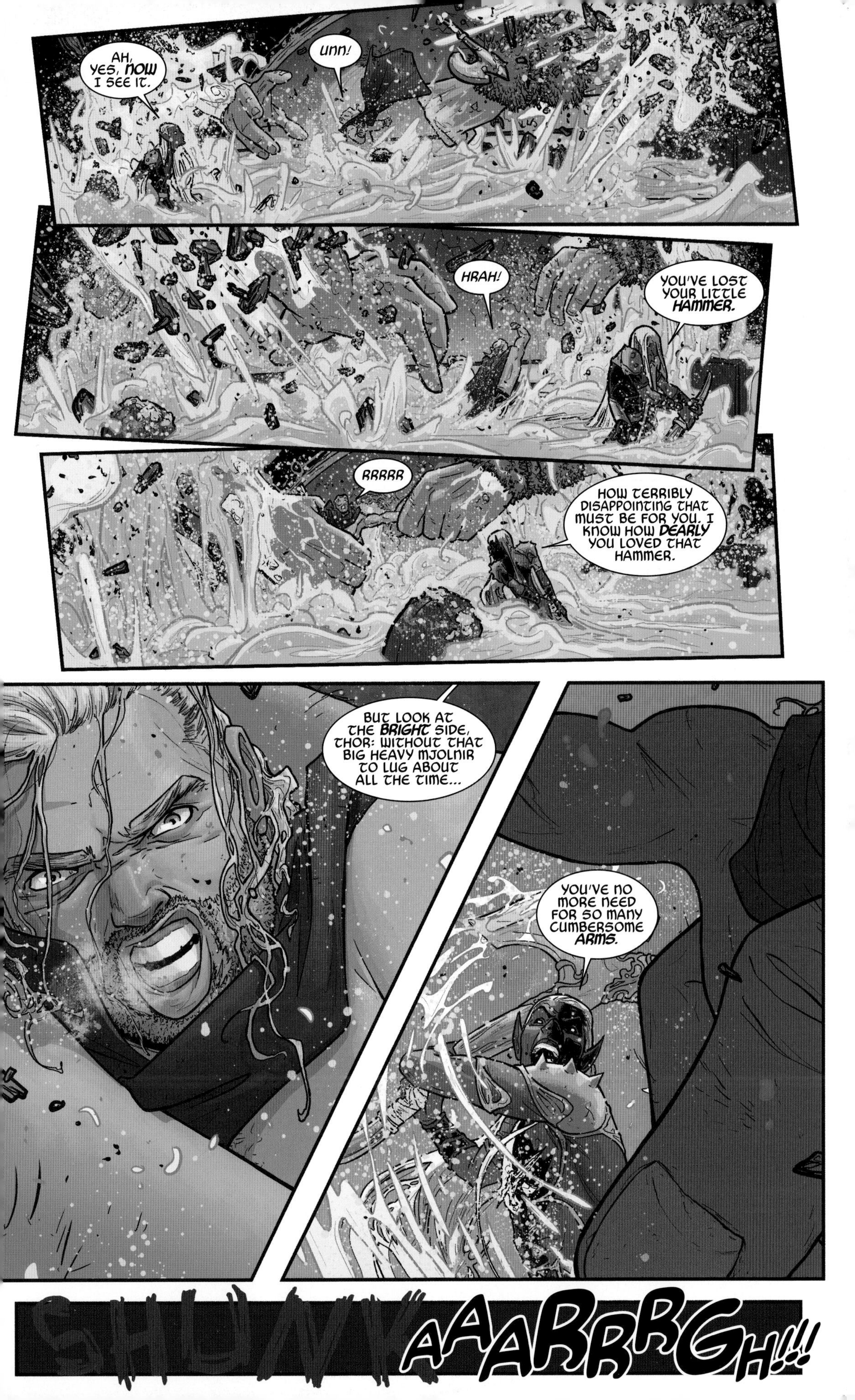
AH, YES, NOW I SEE IT.
UNN!
HRAH!
YOU'VE LOST YOUR LITTLE HAMMER.
RRRRR
HOW TERRIBLY DISAPPOINTING THAT MUST BE FOR YOU. I KNOW HOW DEARLY YOU LOVED THAT HAMMER.
BUT LOOK AT THE BRIGHT SIDE, THOR: WITHOUT THAT BIG HEAVY MJOLNIR TO LUG ABOUT ALL THE TIME...
YOU'VE NO MORE NEED FOR SO MANY CUMBERSOME ARMS.
SHUNNK
AAARRRGH!!!

GLUG

I SEE YOU *FOUND* WHAT I WAS SEARCHING FOR. WELL DONE.

BREATHE EASY NOW, FRIEND. I MEAN YOU NO FURTHER HARM.

FROST GIANTS! NEVER LET IT BE SAID THAT MALEKITH IS NOT AN ELF OF HIS WORD! I HAVE LOCATED YOUR *PRIZE!*

COME, THERE IS MUCH MORE OF MIDGARD FOR YOU TO FREEZE AND FLATTEN!

AND WHAT OF THE GODLING?

ALAS, HE WILL NOT BE JOINING US. I DARE SAY...

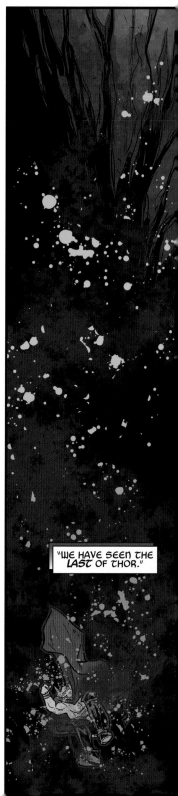

"WE HAVE SEEN THE *LAST* OF THOR."

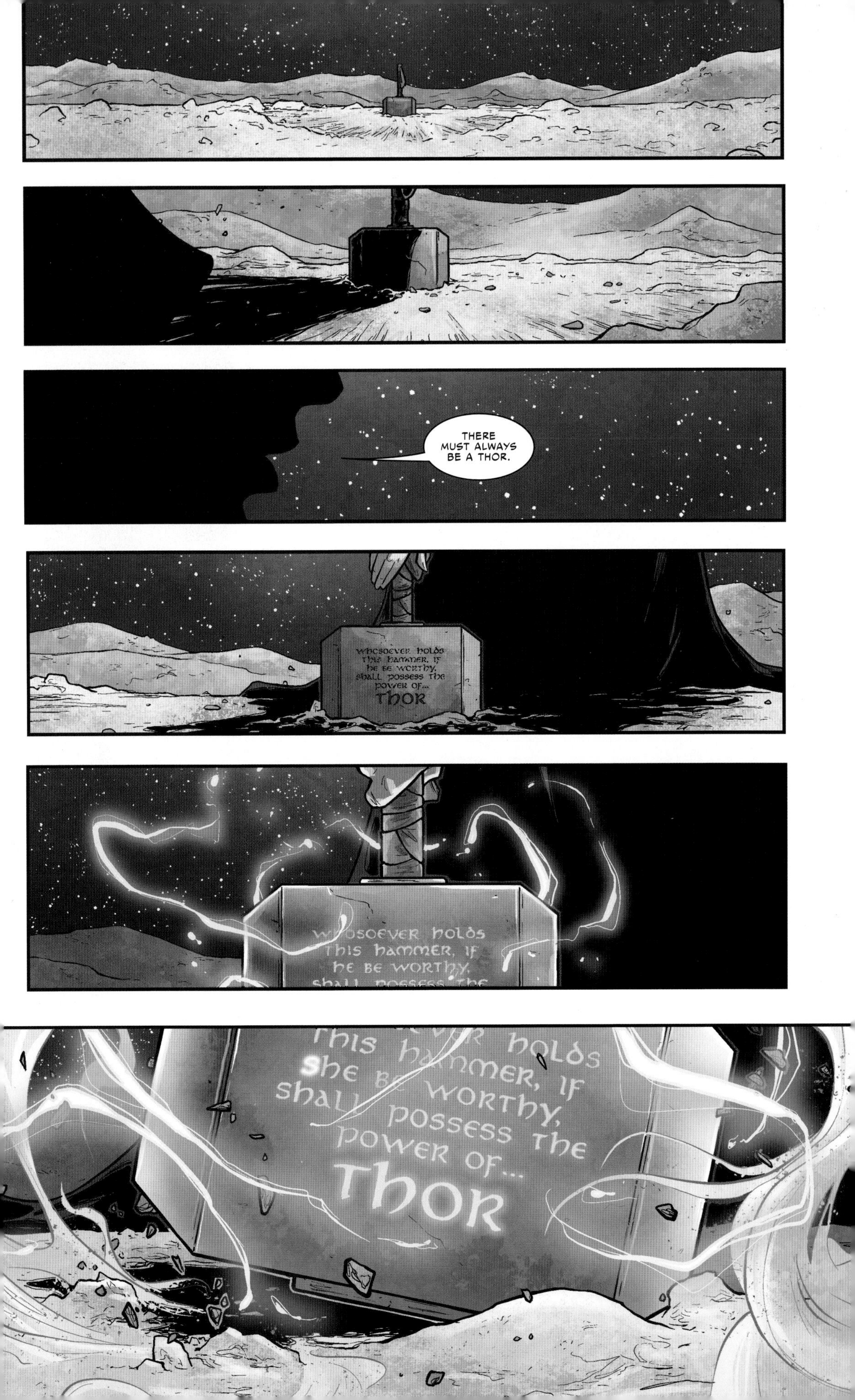
THERE MUST ALWAYS BE A THOR.
whosoever holds this hammer, if he be worthy, shall possess the power of... THOR
whosoever holds this hammer, if he be worthy,
holds
this hammer, if
she be worthy,
shall possess the
power of...
THOR

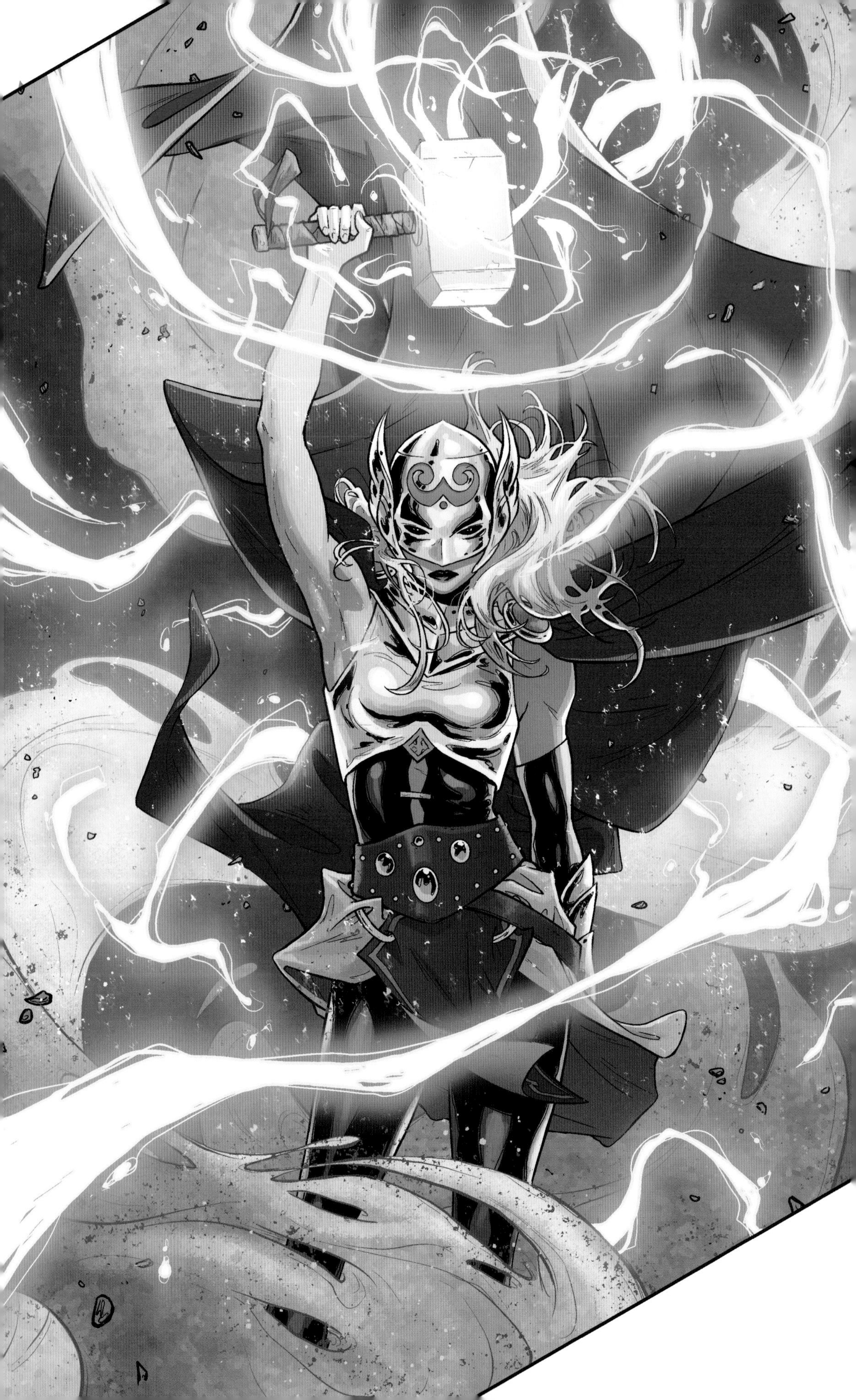

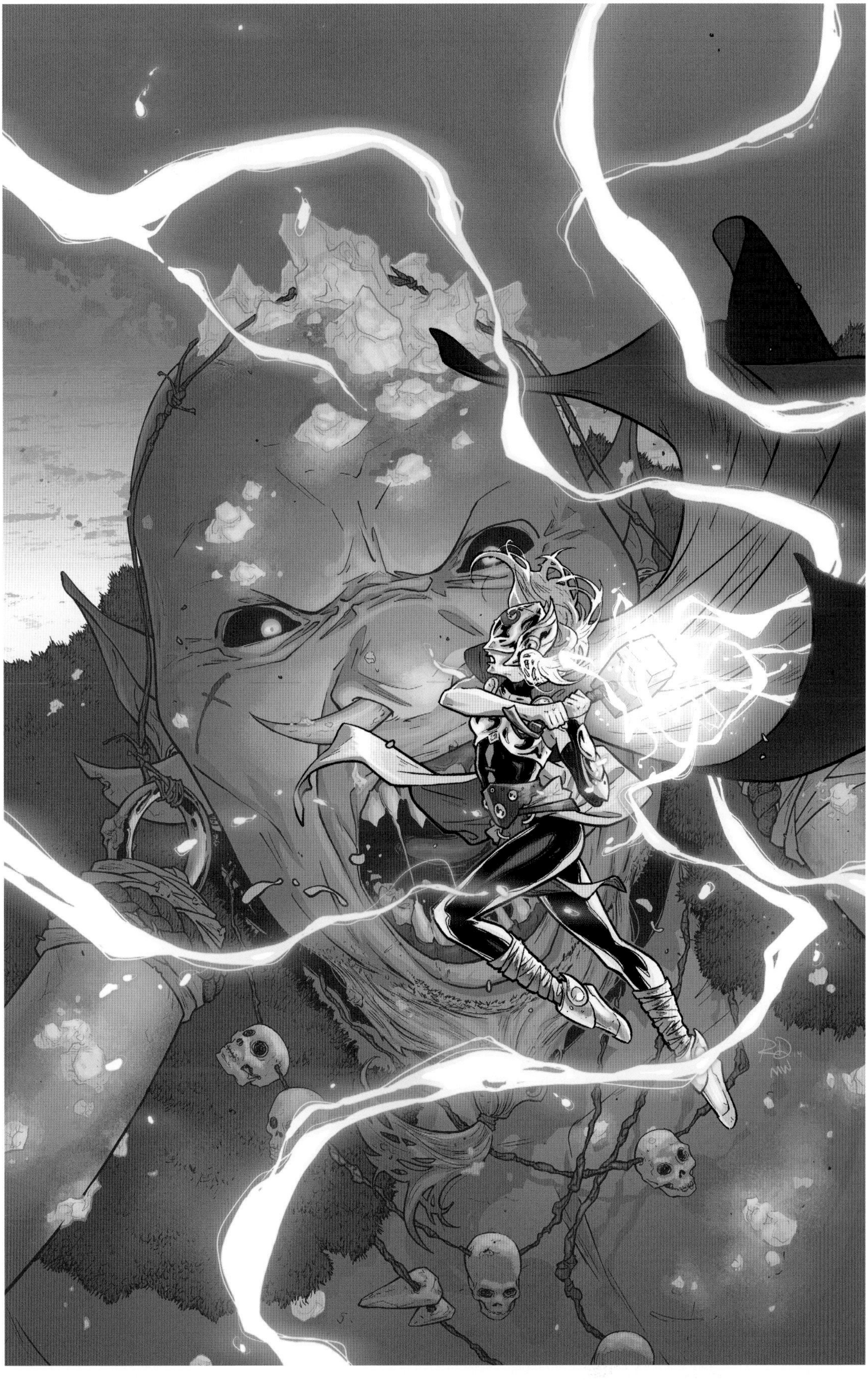

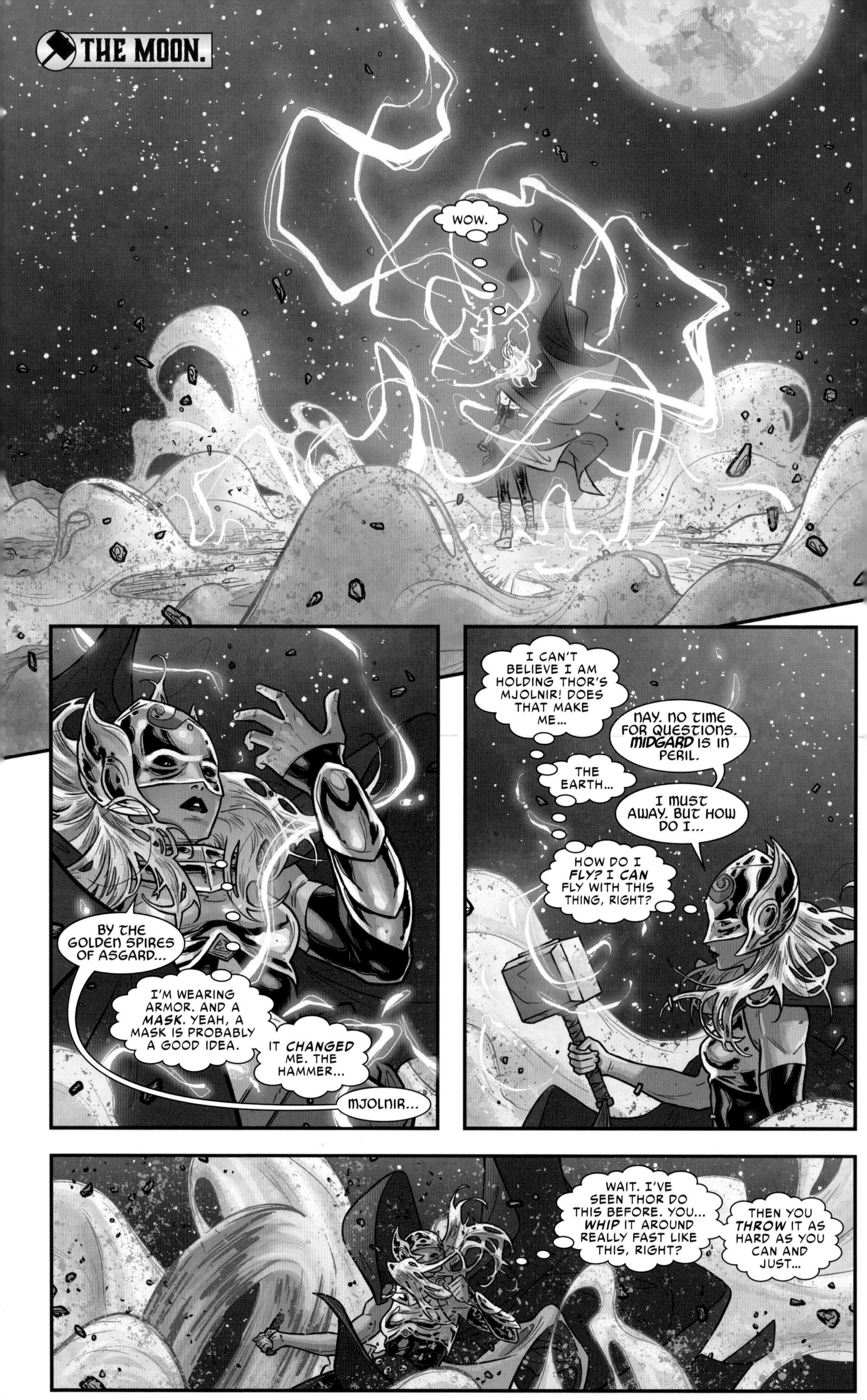
THE MOON.
WOW.
BY THE GOLDEN SPIRES OF ASGARD...
MJOLNIR...
I'M WEARING ARMOR. AND A MASK. YEAH, A MASK IS PROBABLY A GOOD IDEA.
IT CHANGED ME. THE HAMMER...
I CAN'T BELIEVE I AM HOLDING THOR'S MJOLNIR! DOES THAT MAKE ME...
THE EARTH...
NAY. NO TIME FOR QUESTIONS. MIDGARD IS IN PERIL.
I MUST AWAY. BUT HOW DO I...
HOW DO I FLY? I CAN FLY WITH THIS THING, RIGHT?
WAIT. I'VE SEEN THOR DO THIS BEFORE. YOU... WHIP IT AROUND REALLY FAST LIKE THIS, RIGHT?
THEN YOU THROW IT AS HARD AS YOU CAN AND JUST...

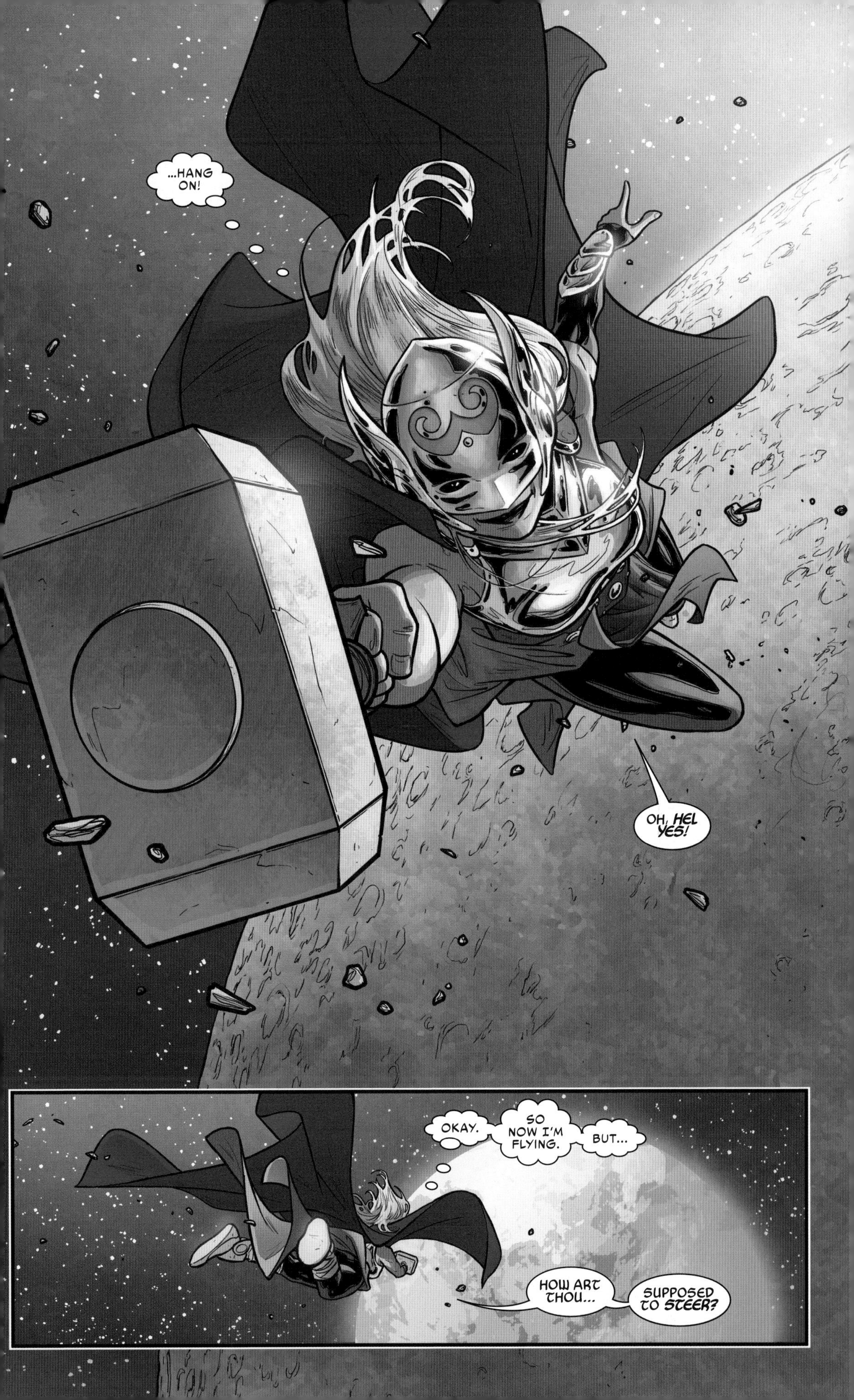
...HANG ON!
OH, HEL YES!
OKAY.
SO NOW I'M FLYING.
BUT...
HOW ART THOU...
SUPPOSED TO STEER?

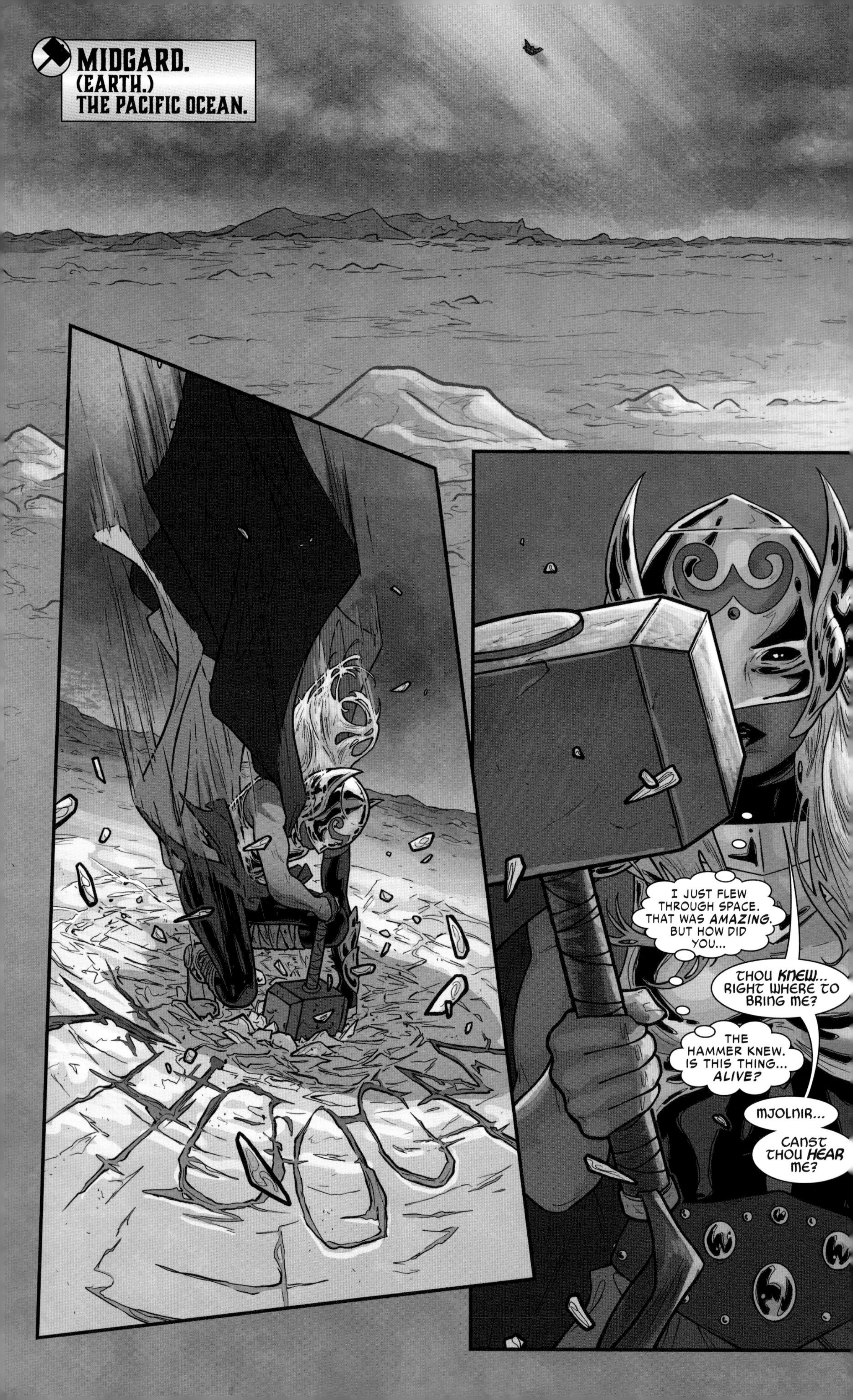
MIDGARD.
(EARTH.)
THE PACIFIC OCEAN.
I JUST FLEW THROUGH SPACE. THAT WAS AMAZING. BUT HOW DID YOU...
THOU KNEW... RIGHT WHERE TO BRING ME?
THE HAMMER KNEW. IS THIS THING... ALIVE?
MJOLNIR...
CANST THOU HEAR ME?

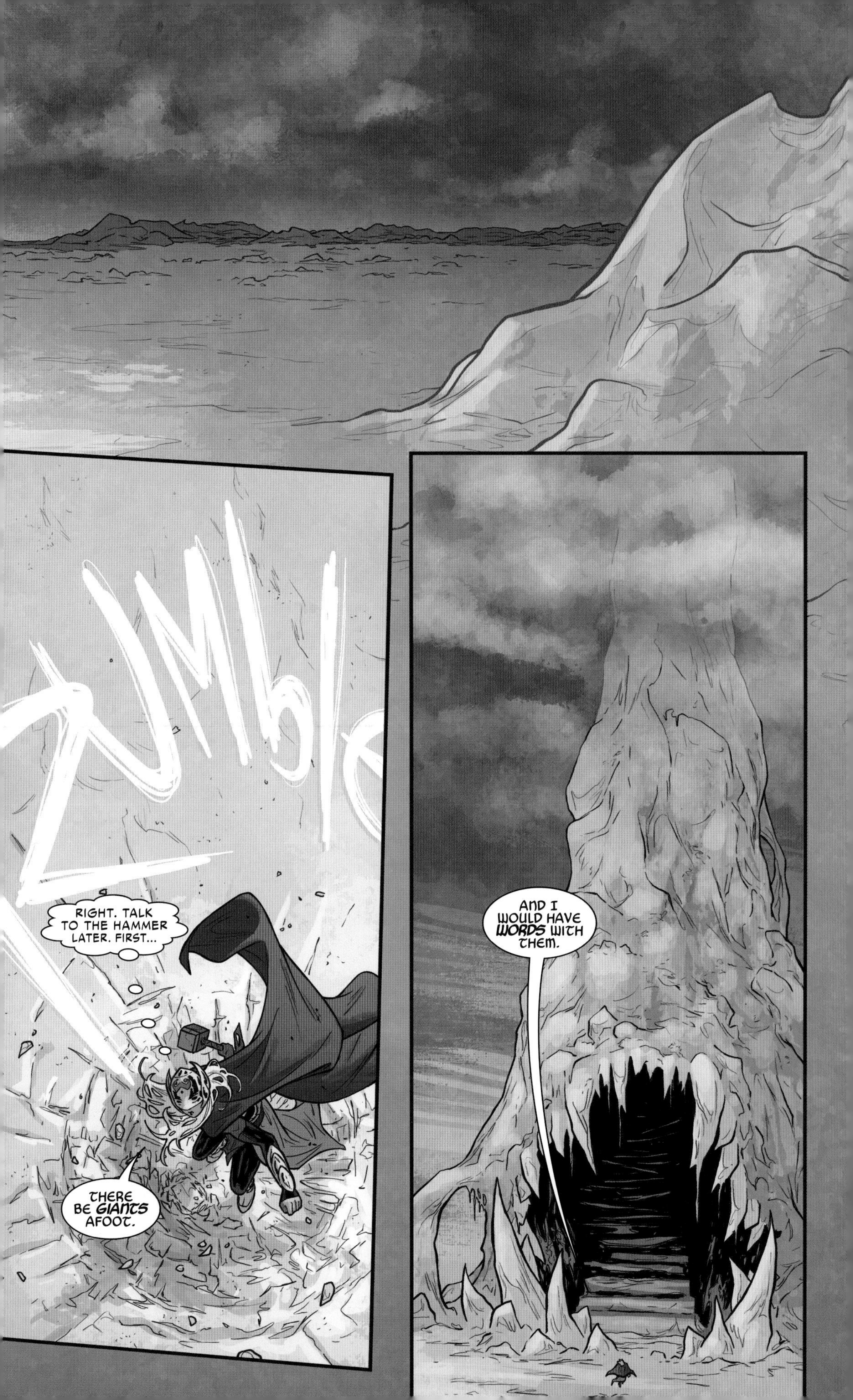
RIGHT. TALK TO THE HAMMER LATER. FIRST...
THERE BE GIANTS AFOOT.
AND I WOULD HAVE WORDS WITH THEM.

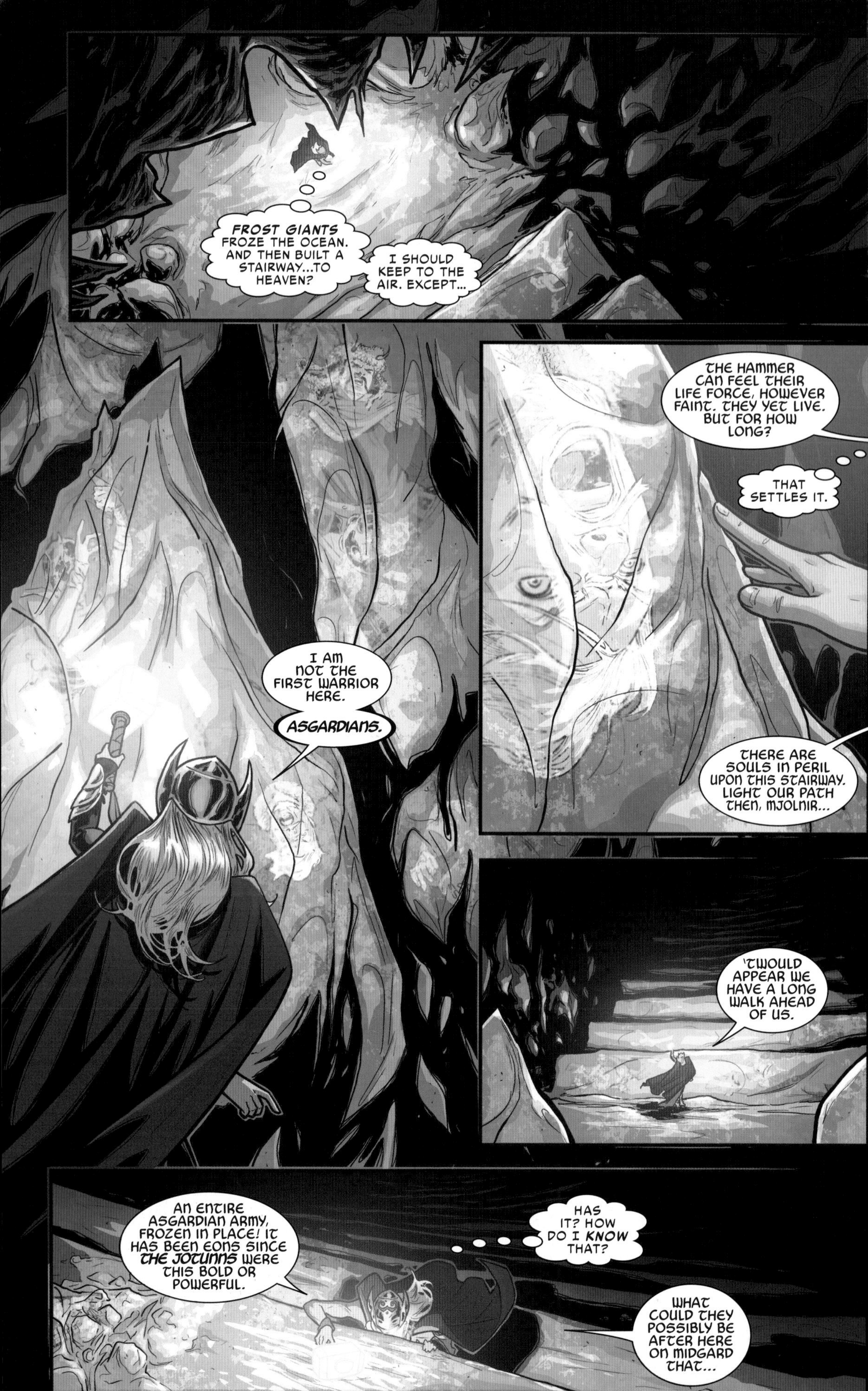

FROST GIANTS FROZE THE OCEAN. AND THEN BUILT A STAIRWAY...TO HEAVEN?
I SHOULD KEEP TO THE AIR. EXCEPT...
I AM NOT THE FIRST WARRIOR HERE.
ASGARDIANS.
THE HAMMER CAN FEEL THEIR LIFE FORCE, HOWEVER FAINT. THEY YET LIVE. BUT FOR HOW LONG?
THAT SETTLES IT.
THERE ARE SOULS IN PERIL UPON THIS STAIRWAY. LIGHT OUR PATH THEN, MJOLNIR...
'TWOULD APPEAR WE HAVE A LONG WALK AHEAD OF US.
AN ENTIRE ASGARDIAN ARMY, FROZEN IN PLACE! IT HAS BEEN EONS SINCE THE JOTUNNS WERE THIS BOLD OR POWERFUL.
HAS IT? HOW DO I KNOW THAT?
WHAT COULD THEY POSSIBLY BE AFTER HERE ON MIDGARD THAT...

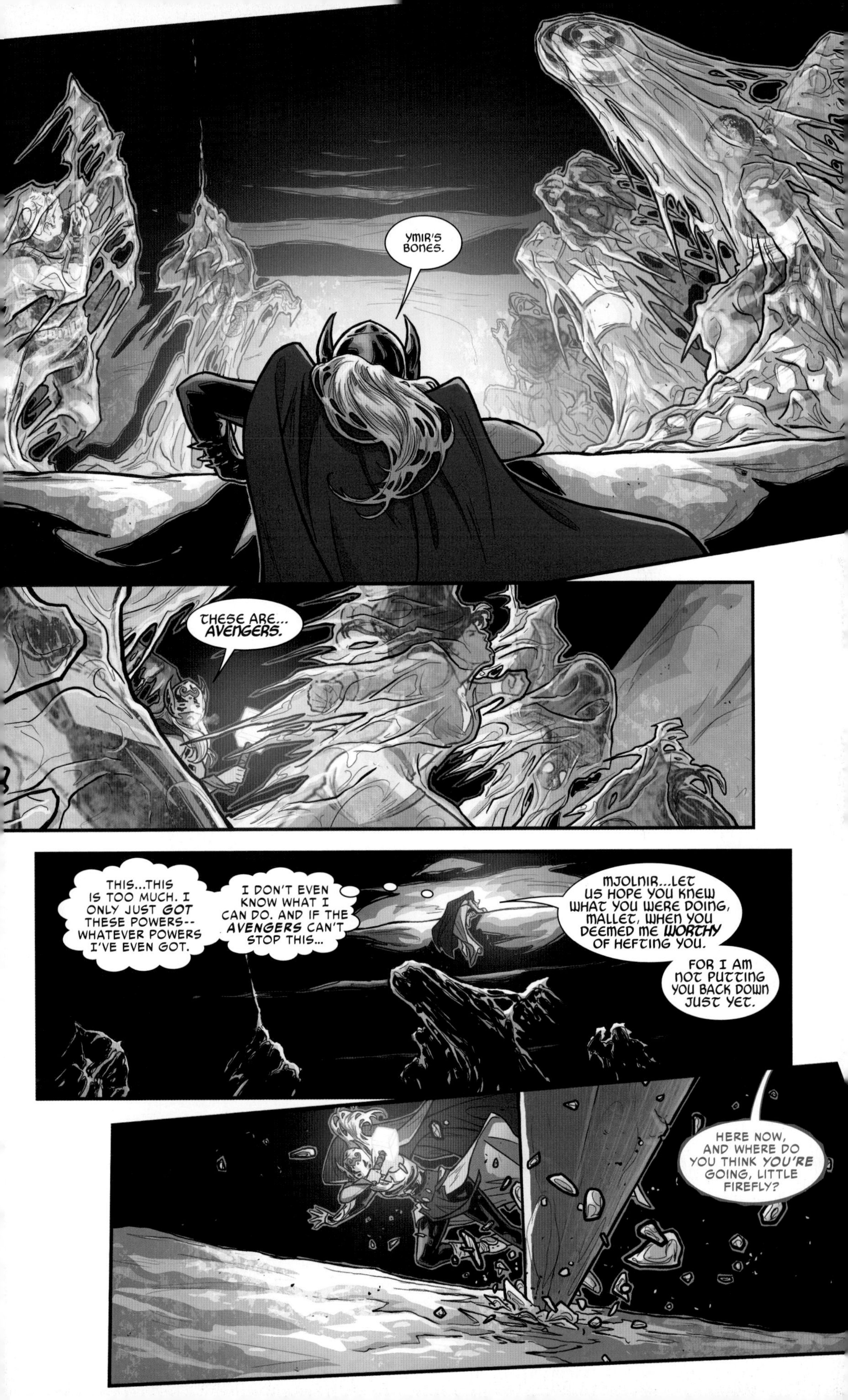
YMIR'S BONES.
THESE ARE... AVENGERS.
THIS...THIS IS TOO MUCH. I ONLY JUST GOT THESE POWERS-- WHATEVER POWERS I'VE EVEN GOT.
I DON'T EVEN KNOW WHAT I CAN DO. AND IF THE AVENGERS CAN'T STOP THIS...
MJOLNIR...LET US HOPE YOU KNEW WHAT YOU WERE DOING, MALLET, WHEN YOU DEEMED ME WORTHY OF HEFTING YOU.
FOR I AM NOT PUTTING YOU BACK DOWN JUST YET.
HERE NOW, AND WHERE DO YOU THINK YOU'RE GOING, LITTLE FIREFLY?

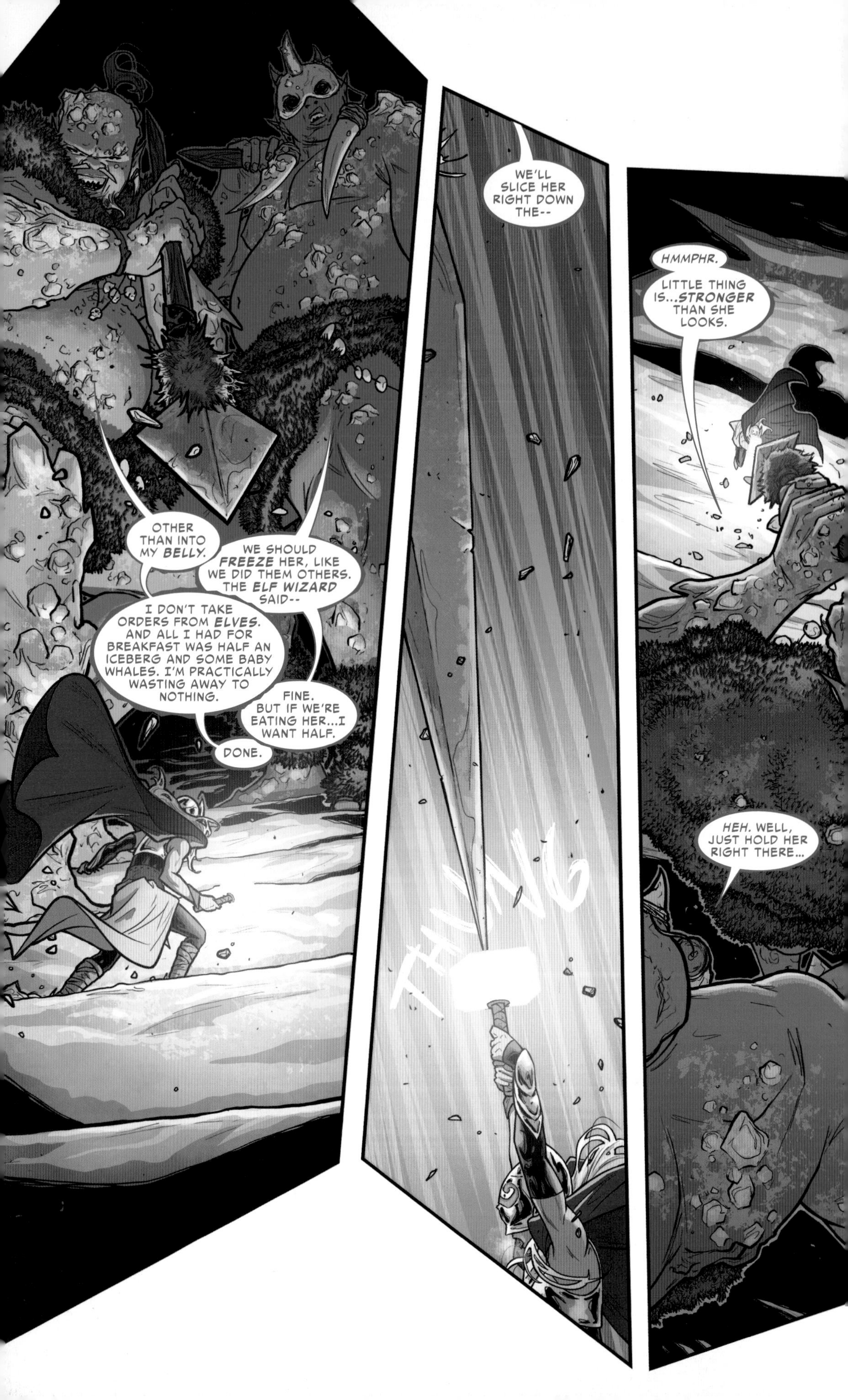
OTHER THAN INTO MY BELLY.
WE SHOULD FREEZE HER, LIKE WE DID THEM OTHERS. THE ELF WIZARD SAID--
I DON'T TAKE ORDERS FROM ELVES. AND ALL I HAD FOR BREAKFAST WAS HALF AN ICEBERG AND SOME BABY WHALES. I'M PRACTICALLY WASTING AWAY TO NOTHING.
FINE. BUT IF WE'RE EATING HER...I WANT HALF.
DONE.
WE'LL SLICE HER RIGHT DOWN THE--
THUNG
HMMPHR.
LITTLE THING IS...STRONGER THAN SHE LOOKS.
HEH. WELL, JUST HOLD HER RIGHT THERE...

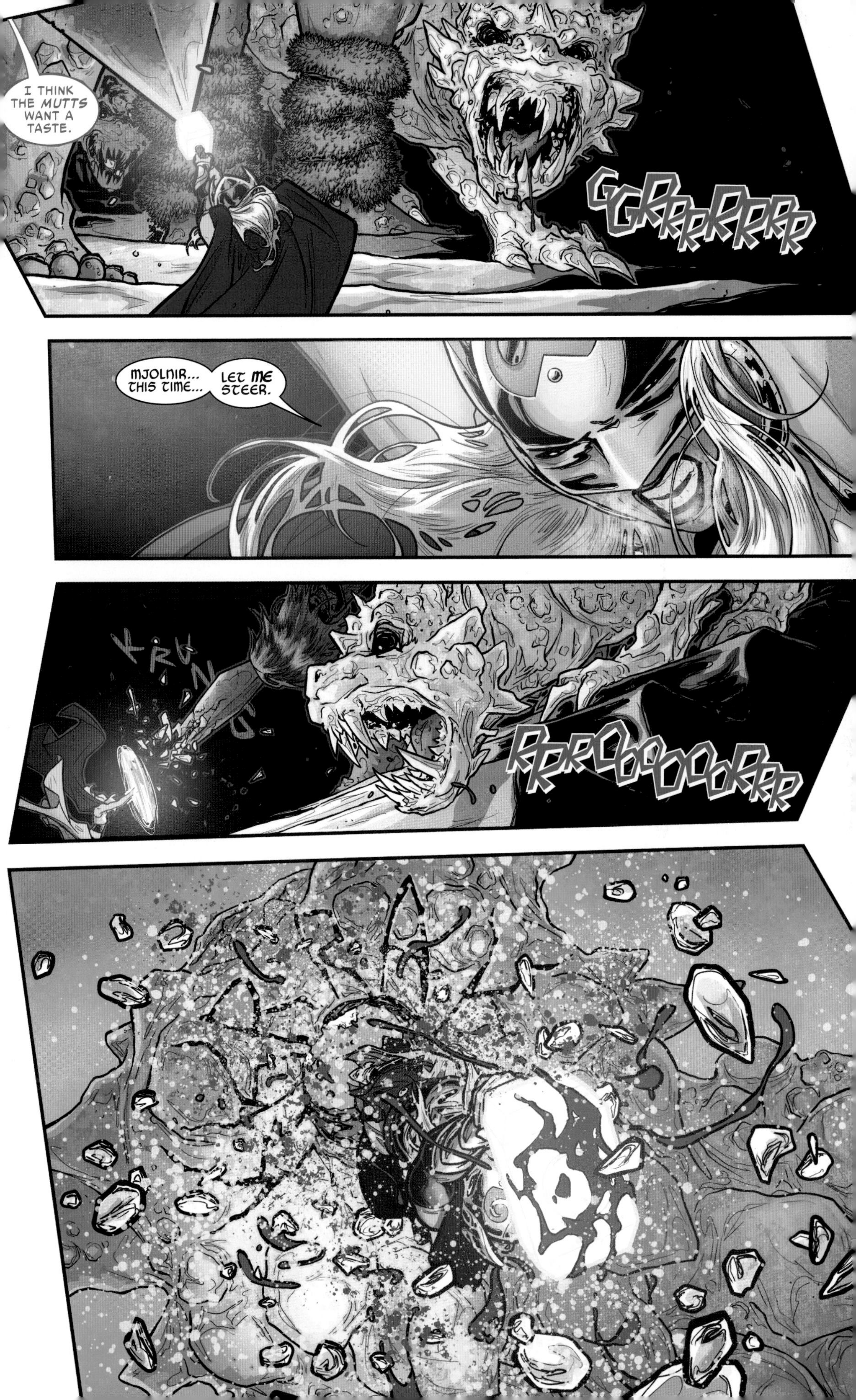
I THINK THE *MUTTS* WANT A TASTE.
GGRRRRRRRRR
MJOLNIR... THIS TIME...
LET *ME* STEER.
KRUNCH
RRRROOOOOORRRR

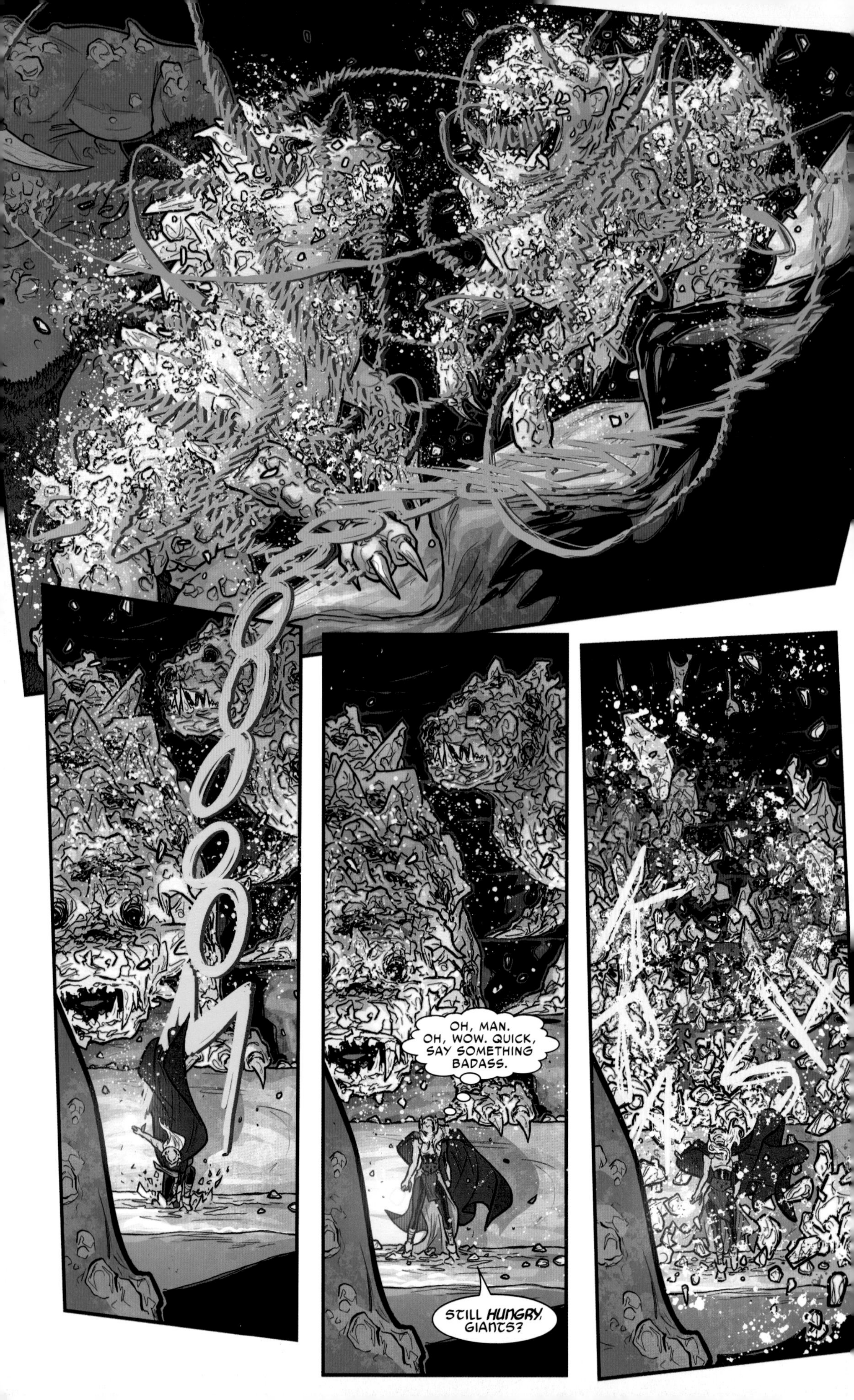
OH, MAN. OH, WOW. QUICK, SAY SOMETHING BADASS.
STILL HUNGRY, GIANTS?

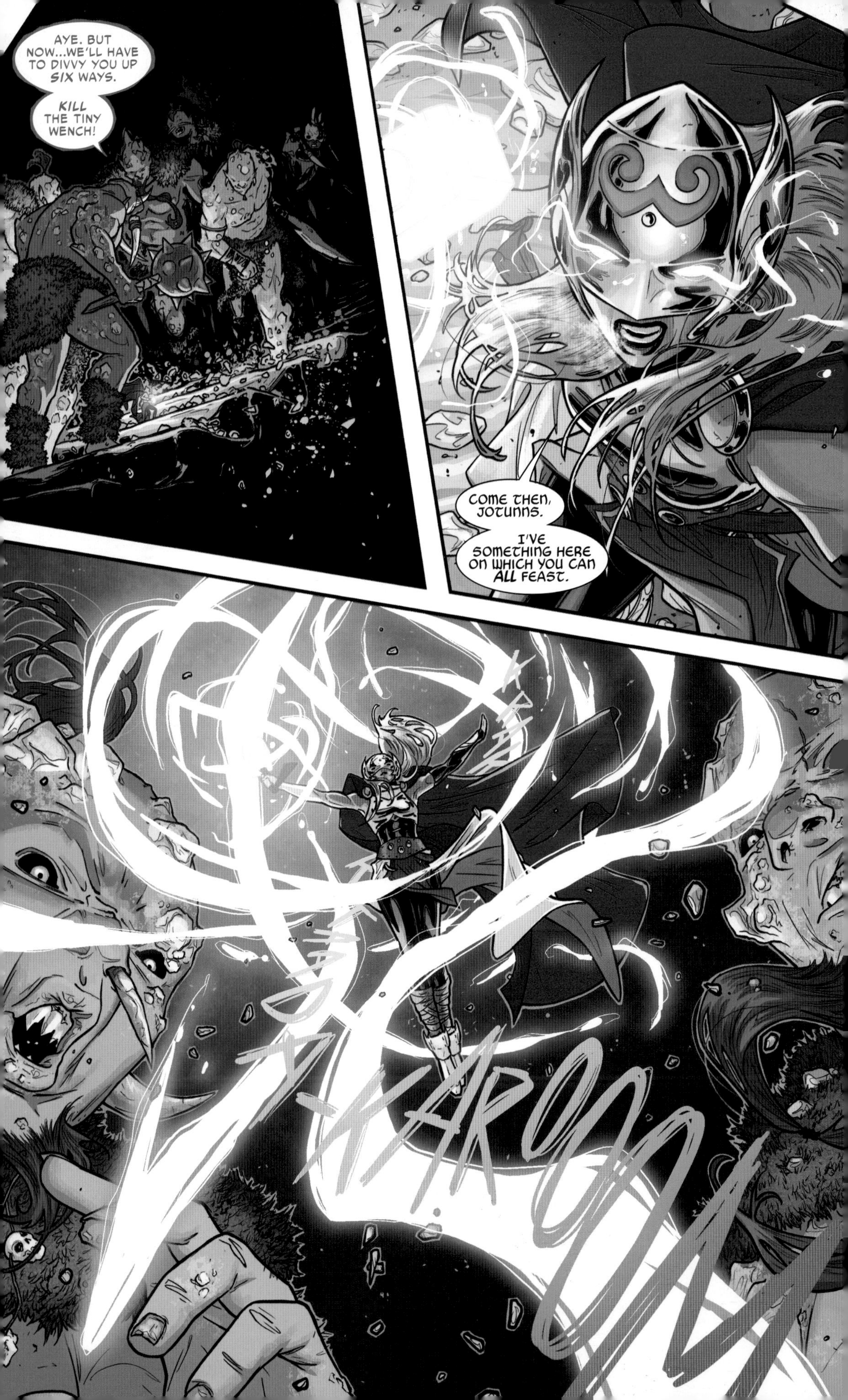
AYE. BUT NOW...WE'LL HAVE TO DIVVY YOU UP SIX WAYS.
KILL THE TINY WENCH!
COME THEN, JOTUNNS.
I'VE SOMETHING HERE ON WHICH YOU CAN ALL FEAST.

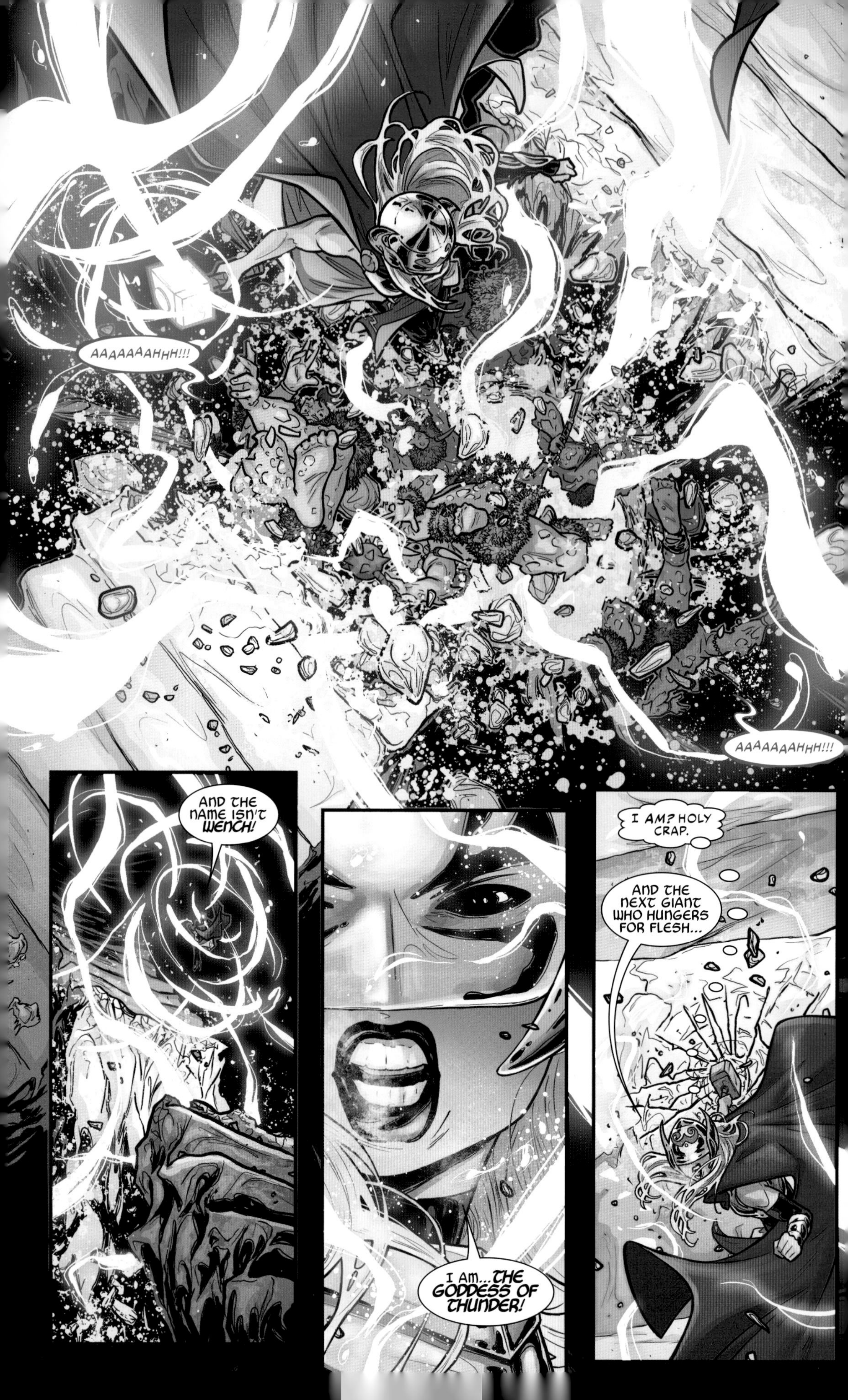
AAAAAAAHHH!!!
AAAAAAAHHH!!!
AND THE NAME ISN'T WENCH!
I AM...THE GODDESS OF THUNDER!
I AM? HOLY CRAP.
AND THE NEXT GIANT WHO HUNGERS FOR FLESH...

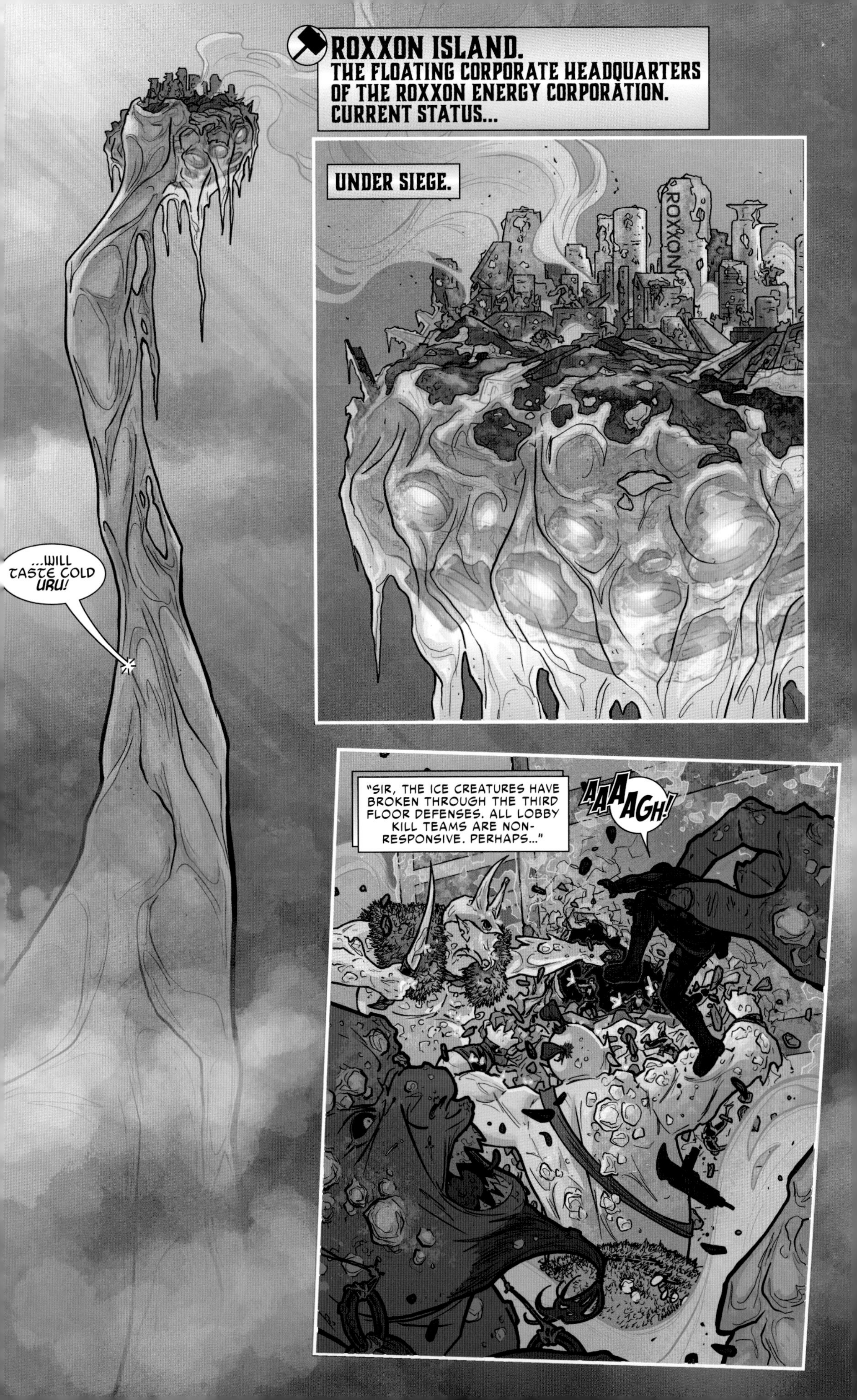
ROXXON ISLAND.
THE FLOATING CORPORATE HEADQUARTERS OF THE ROXXON ENERGY CORPORATION. CURRENT STATUS...
UNDER SIEGE.
ROXXON
...WILL TASTE COLD URU!
"SIR, THE ICE CREATURES HAVE BROKEN THROUGH THE THIRD FLOOR DEFENSES. ALL LOBBY KILL TEAMS ARE NON-RESPONSIVE. PERHAPS..."
AAAAGH!

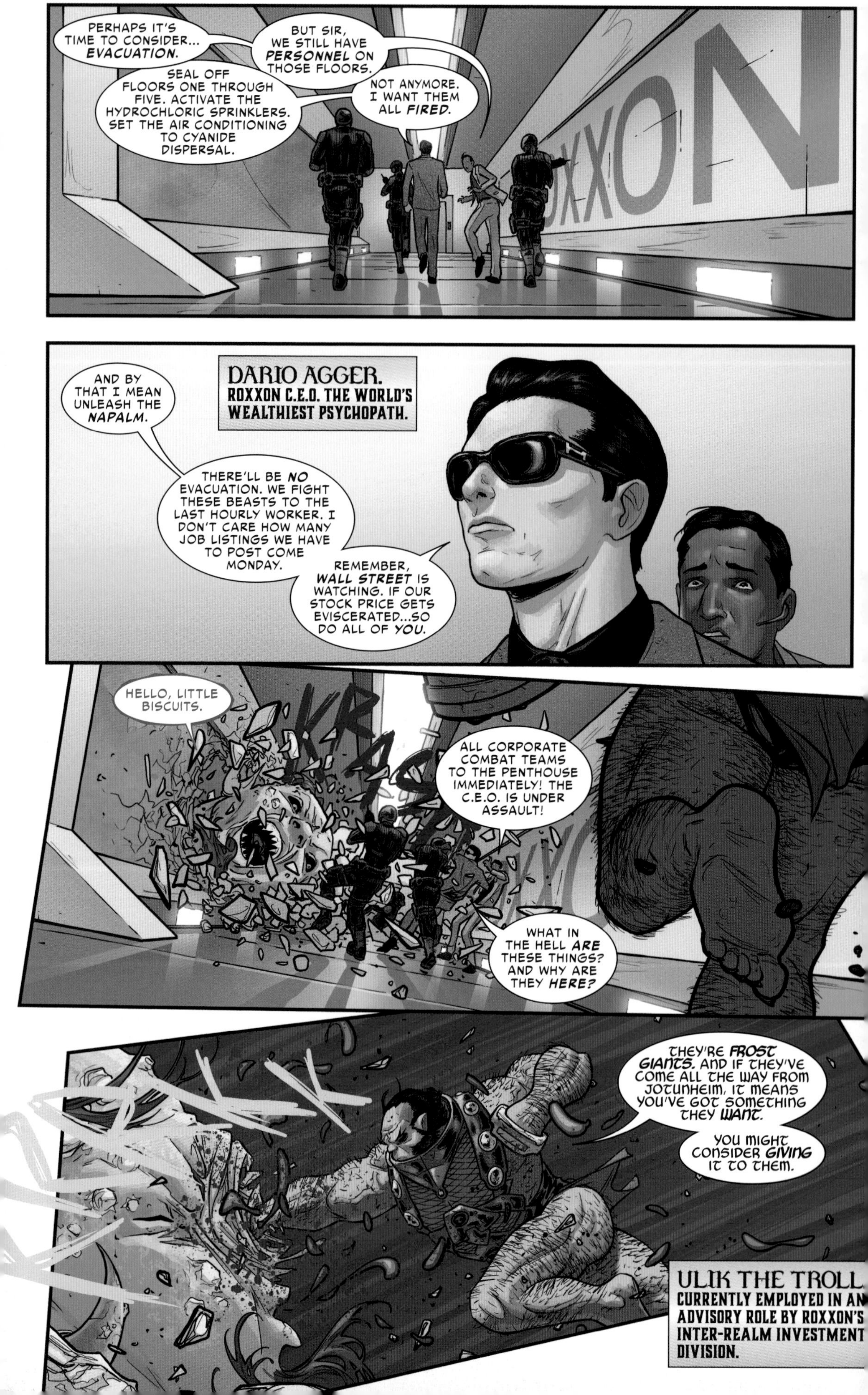
PERHAPS IT'S TIME TO CONSIDER... EVACUATION.
BUT SIR, WE STILL HAVE PERSONNEL ON THOSE FLOORS.
SEAL OFF FLOORS ONE THROUGH FIVE. ACTIVATE THE HYDROCHLORIC SPRINKLERS. SET THE AIR CONDITIONING TO CYANIDE DISPERSAL.
NOT ANYMORE. I WANT THEM ALL FIRED.
ROXXON
DARIO AGGER. ROXXON C.E.O. THE WORLD'S WEALTHIEST PSYCHOPATH.
AND BY THAT I MEAN UNLEASH THE NAPALM.
THERE'LL BE NO EVACUATION. WE FIGHT THESE BEASTS TO THE LAST HOURLY WORKER. I DON'T CARE HOW MANY JOB LISTINGS WE HAVE TO POST COME MONDAY.
REMEMBER, WALL STREET IS WATCHING. IF OUR STOCK PRICE GETS EVISCERATED...SO DO ALL OF YOU.
HELLO, LITTLE BISCUITS.
KRASSH
ALL CORPORATE COMBAT TEAMS TO THE PENTHOUSE IMMEDIATELY! THE C.E.O. IS UNDER ASSAULT!
WHAT IN THE HELL ARE THESE THINGS? AND WHY ARE THEY HERE?
THEY'RE FROST GIANTS. AND IF THEY'VE COME ALL THE WAY FROM JOTUNHEIM, IT MEANS YOU'VE GOT SOMETHING THEY WANT.
YOU MIGHT CONSIDER GIVING IT TO THEM.
ULIK THE TROLL. CURRENTLY EMPLOYED IN AN ADVISORY ROLE BY ROXXON'S INTER-REALM INVESTMENT DIVISION.

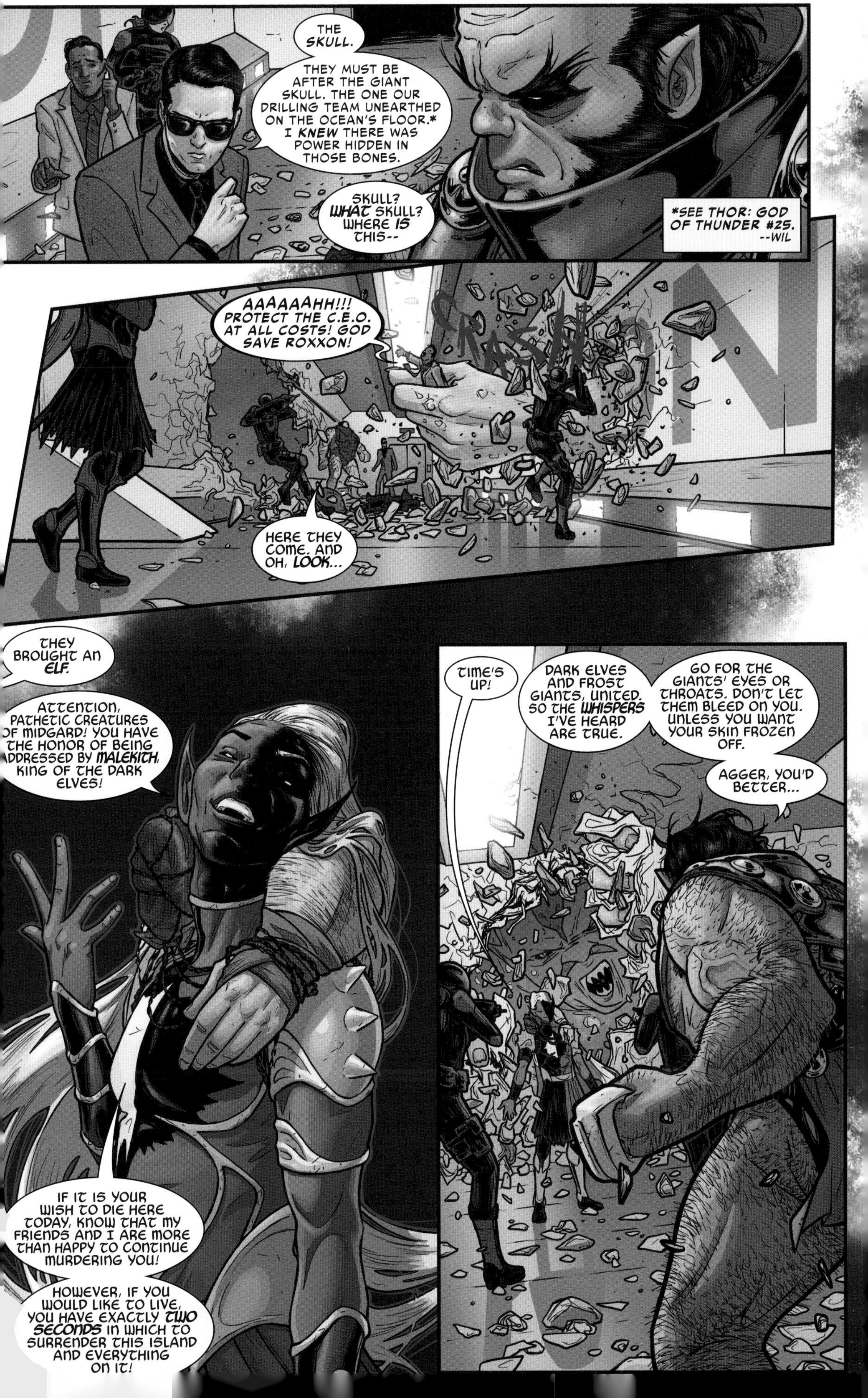
THE SKULL.
THEY MUST BE AFTER THE GIANT SKULL. THE ONE OUR DRILLING TEAM UNEARTHED ON THE OCEAN'S FLOOR.* I KNEW THERE WAS POWER HIDDEN IN THOSE BONES.
SKULL? WHAT SKULL? WHERE IS THIS--
*SEE THOR: GOD OF THUNDER #25. --WIL
AAAAAAHH!!! PROTECT THE C.E.O. AT ALL COSTS! GOD SAVE ROXXON!
CRASH
HERE THEY COME. AND OH, LOOK...
THEY BROUGHT AN ELF.
ATTENTION, PATHETIC CREATURES OF MIDGARD! YOU HAVE THE HONOR OF BEING ADDRESSED BY MALEKITH, KING OF THE DARK ELVES!
IF IT IS YOUR WISH TO DIE HERE TODAY, KNOW THAT MY FRIENDS AND I ARE MORE THAN HAPPY TO CONTINUE MURDERING YOU!
HOWEVER, IF YOU WOULD LIKE TO LIVE, YOU HAVE EXACTLY TWO SECONDS IN WHICH TO SURRENDER THIS ISLAND AND EVERYTHING ON IT!
TIME'S UP!
DARK ELVES AND FROST GIANTS, UNITED. SO THE WHISPERS I'VE HEARD ARE TRUE.
GO FOR THE GIANTS' EYES OR THROATS. DON'T LET THEM BLEED ON YOU. UNLESS YOU WANT YOUR SKIN FROZEN OFF.
AGGER, YOU'D BETTER...

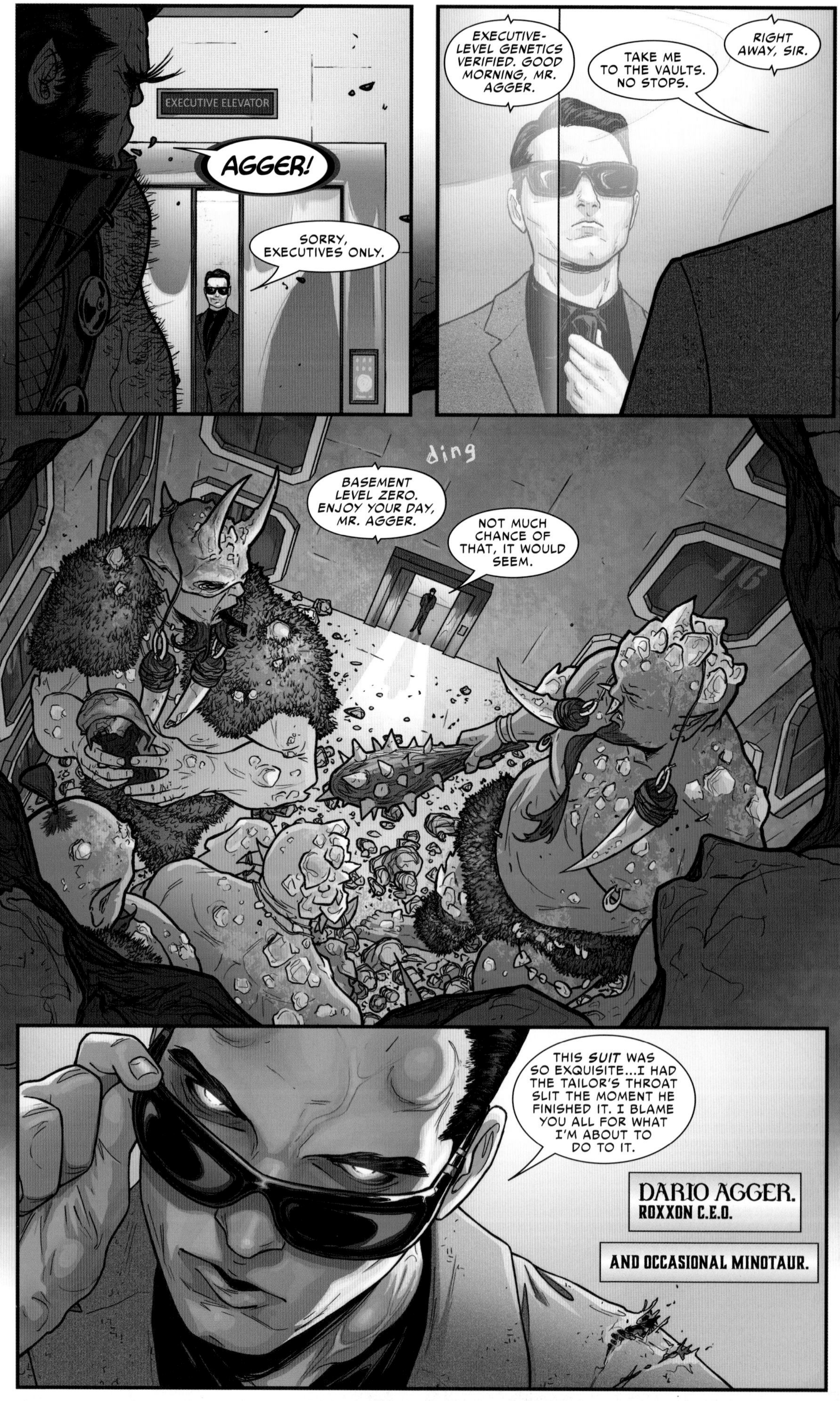
EXECUTIVE ELEVATOR
AGGER!
SORRY, EXECUTIVES ONLY.
EXECUTIVE-LEVEL GENETICS VERIFIED. GOOD MORNING, MR. AGGER.
TAKE ME TO THE VAULTS. NO STOPS.
RIGHT AWAY, SIR.
ding
BASEMENT LEVEL ZERO. ENJOY YOUR DAY, MR. AGGER.
NOT MUCH CHANCE OF THAT, IT WOULD SEEM.
THIS SUIT WAS SO EXQUISITE...I HAD THE TAILOR'S THROAT SLIT THE MOMENT HE FINISHED IT. I BLAME YOU ALL FOR WHAT I'M ABOUT TO DO TO IT.
DARIO AGGER. ROXXON C.E.O.
AND OCCASIONAL MINOTAUR.

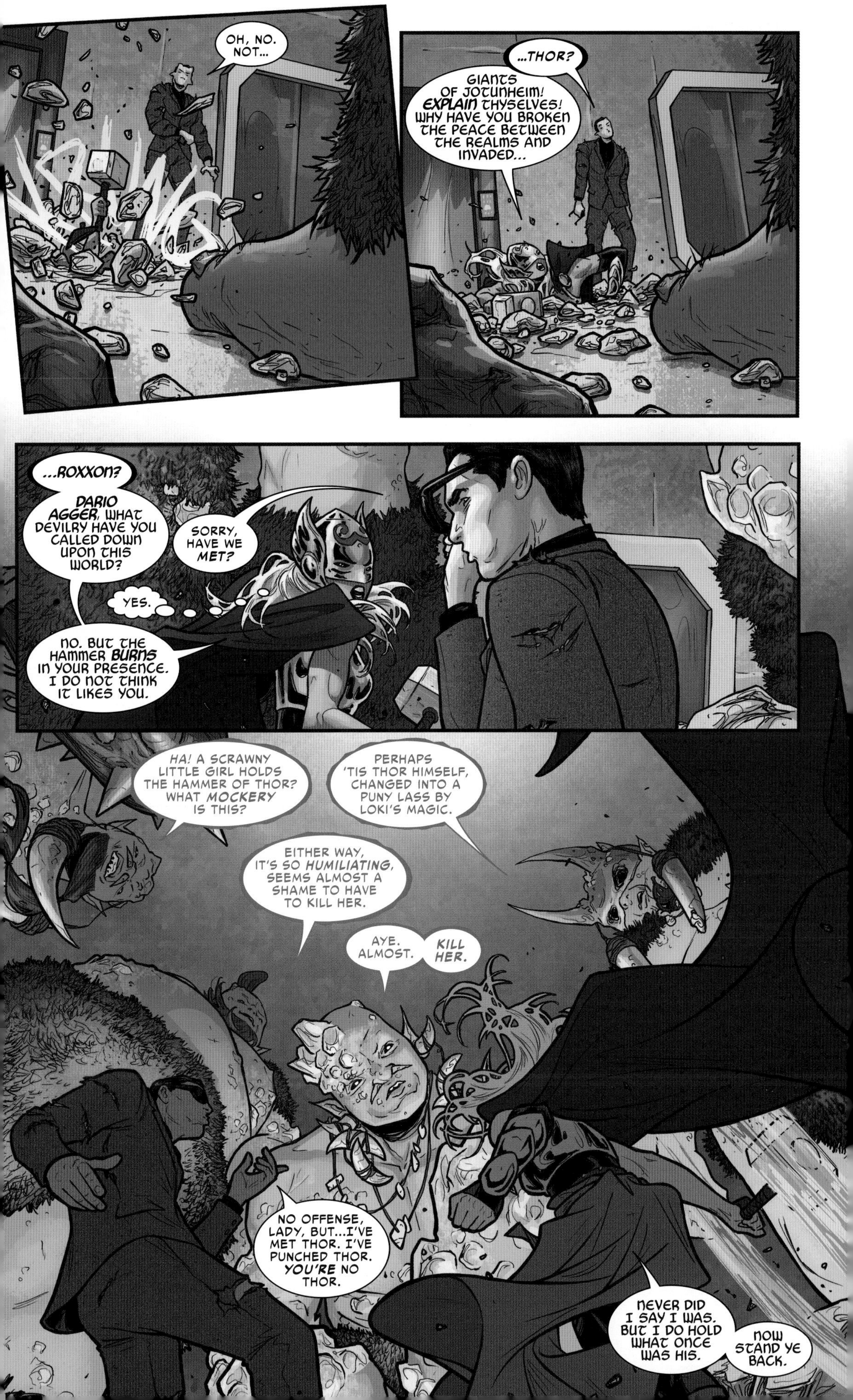
OH, NO. NOT...
...THOR?
GIANTS OF JOTUNHEIM! EXPLAIN THYSELVES! WHY HAVE YOU BROKEN THE PEACE BETWEEN THE REALMS AND INVADED...
...ROXXON?
DARIO AGGER, WHAT DEVILRY HAVE YOU CALLED DOWN UPON THIS WORLD?
SORRY, HAVE WE MET?
YES.
NO. BUT THE HAMMER BURNS IN YOUR PRESENCE. I DO NOT THINK IT LIKES YOU.
HA! A SCRAWNY LITTLE GIRL HOLDS THE HAMMER OF THOR? WHAT MOCKERY IS THIS?
PERHAPS 'TIS THOR HIMSELF, CHANGED INTO A PUNY LASS BY LOKI'S MAGIC.
EITHER WAY, IT'S SO HUMILIATING, SEEMS ALMOST A SHAME TO HAVE TO KILL HER.
AYE. ALMOST.
KILL HER.
NO OFFENSE, LADY, BUT...I'VE MET THOR. I'VE PUNCHED THOR. YOU'RE NO THOR.
NEVER DID I SAY I WAS. BUT I DO HOLD WHAT ONCE WAS HIS.
NOW STAND YE BACK.

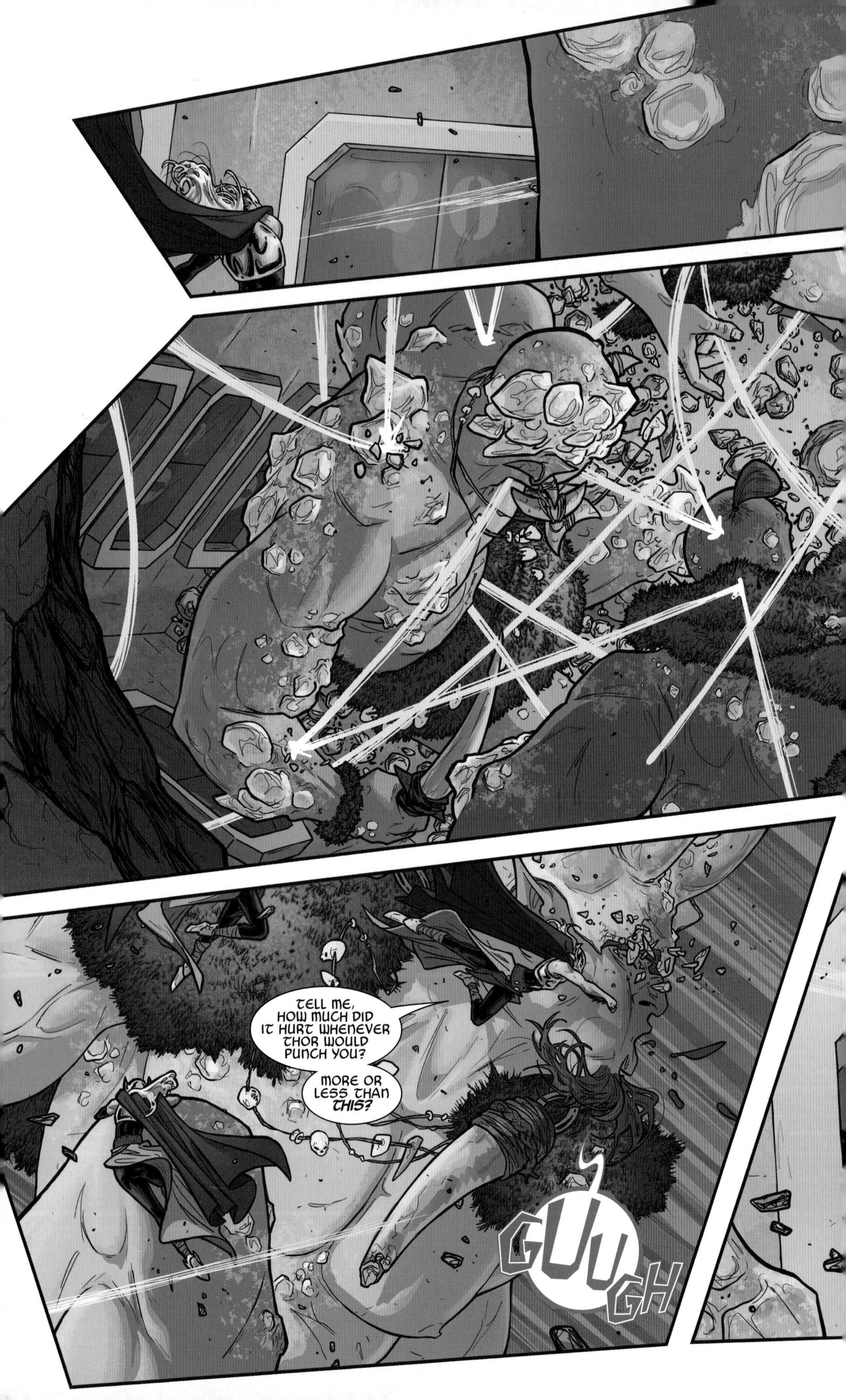
TELL ME, HOW MUCH DID IT HURT WHENEVER THOR WOULD PUNCH YOU?
MORE OR LESS THAN *THIS?*
GUUGH

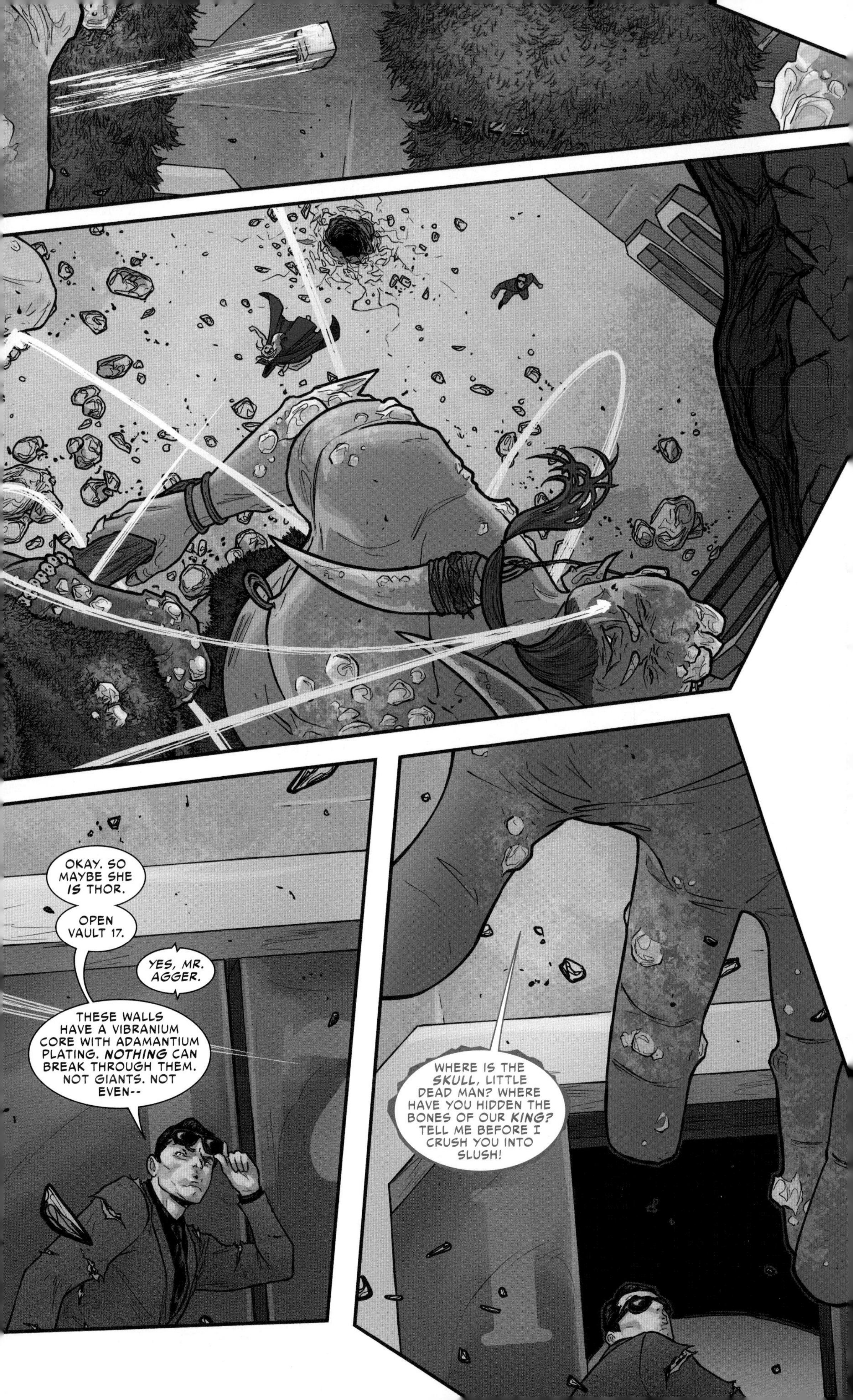
OKAY. SO MAYBE SHE *IS* THOR.
OPEN VAULT 17.
YES, MR. AGGER.
THESE WALLS HAVE A VIBRANIUM CORE WITH ADAMANTIUM PLATING. *NOTHING* CAN BREAK THROUGH THEM. NOT GIANTS. NOT EVEN--
WHERE IS THE *SKULL*, LITTLE DEAD MAN? WHERE HAVE YOU HIDDEN THE BONES OF OUR *KING?* TELL ME BEFORE I CRUSH YOU INTO SLUSH!

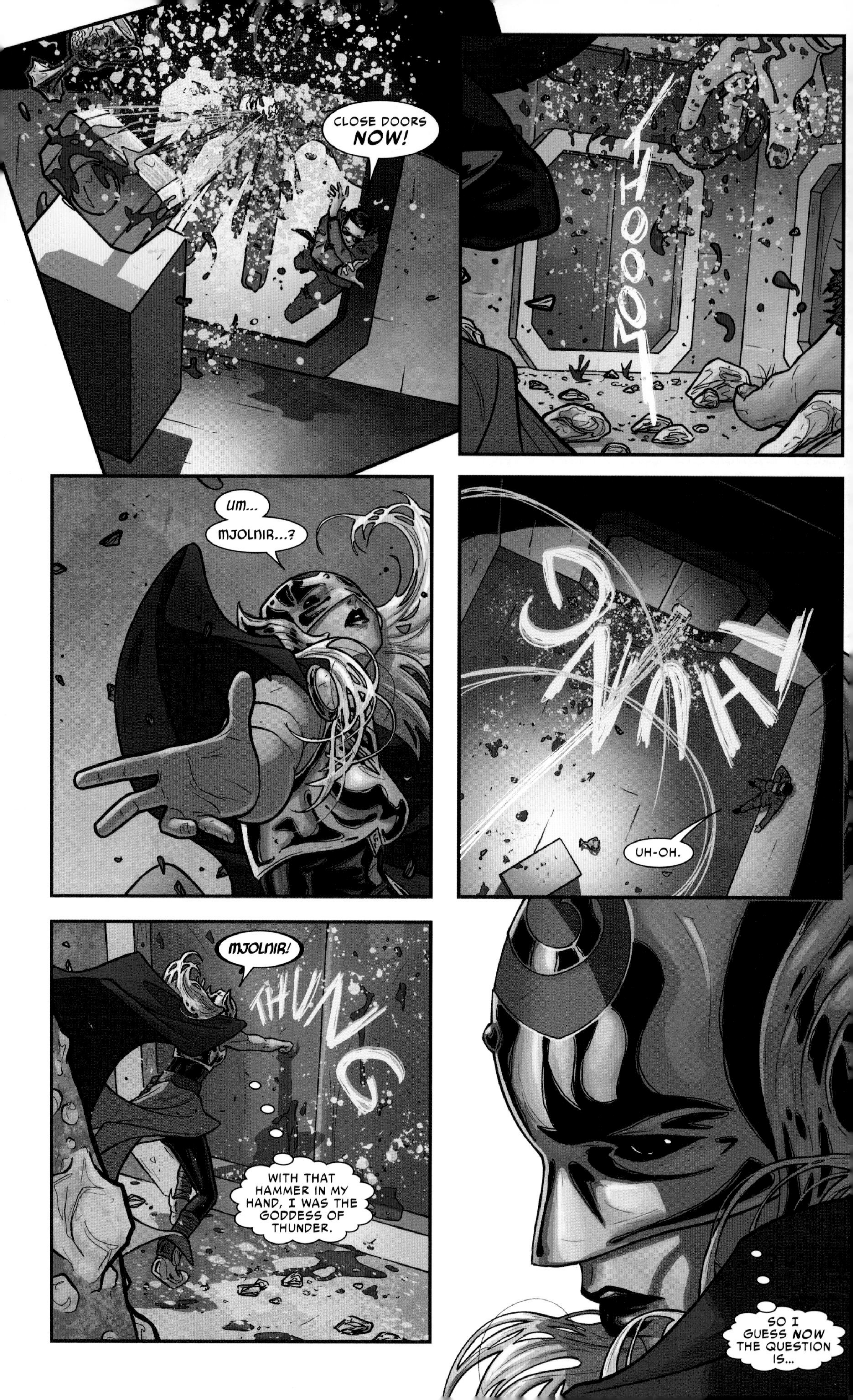
CLOSE DOORS NOW!
THOOOOM
UM...
MJOLNIR...?
UH-OH.
MJOLNIR!
THUNG
WITH THAT HAMMER IN MY HAND, I WAS THE GODDESS OF THUNDER.
SO I GUESS NOW THE QUESTION IS...

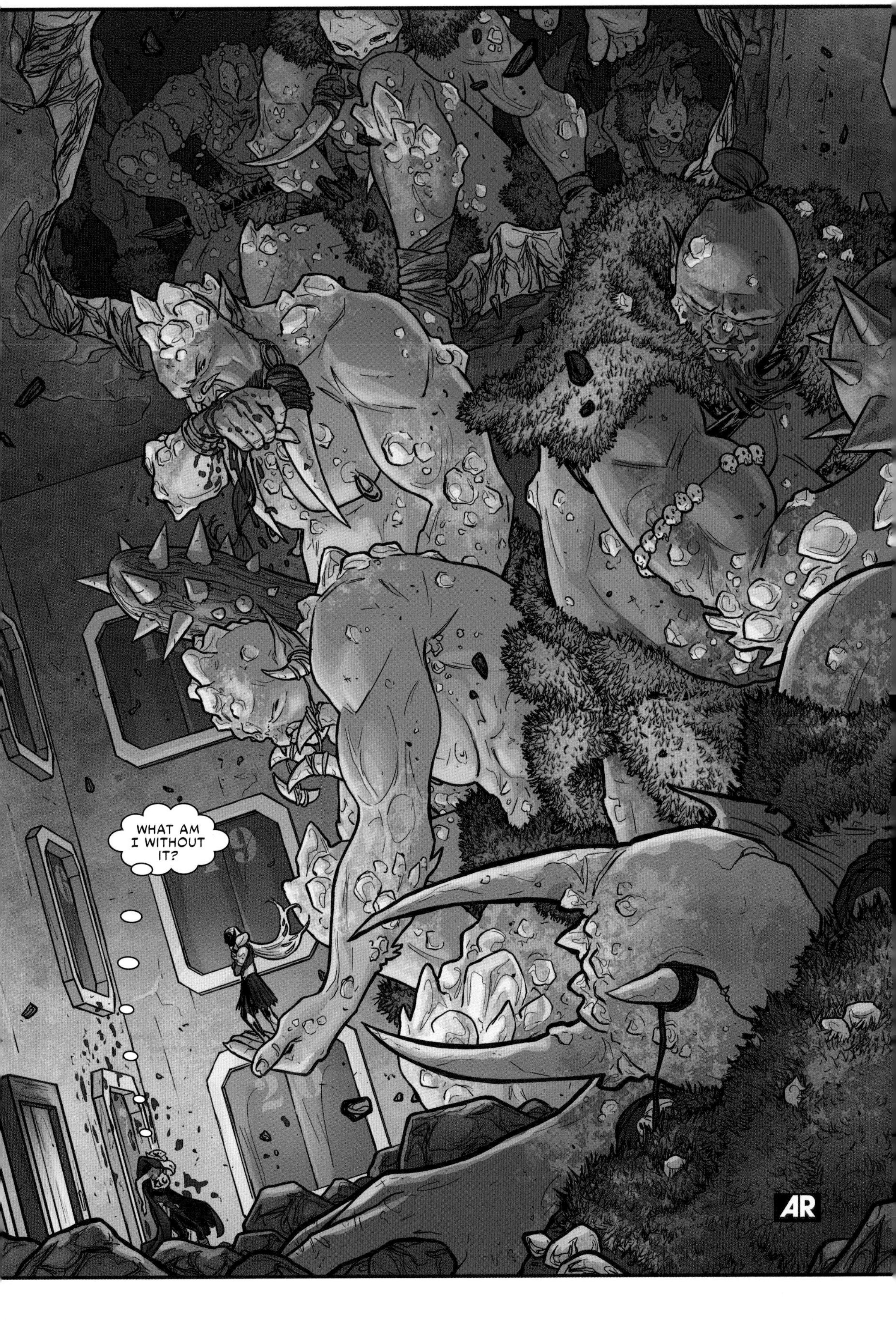
WHAT AM I WITHOUT IT?
AR

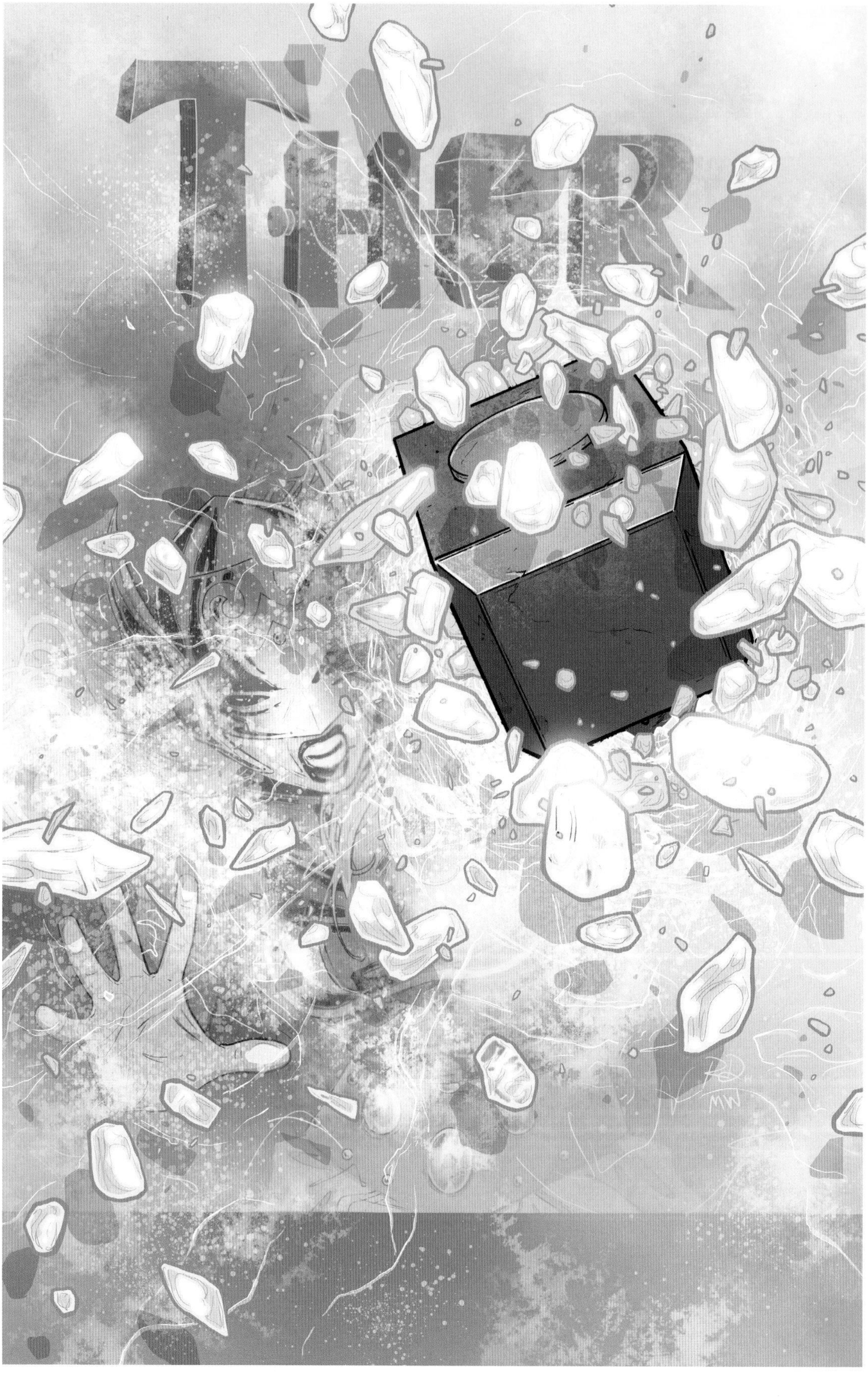
THOR

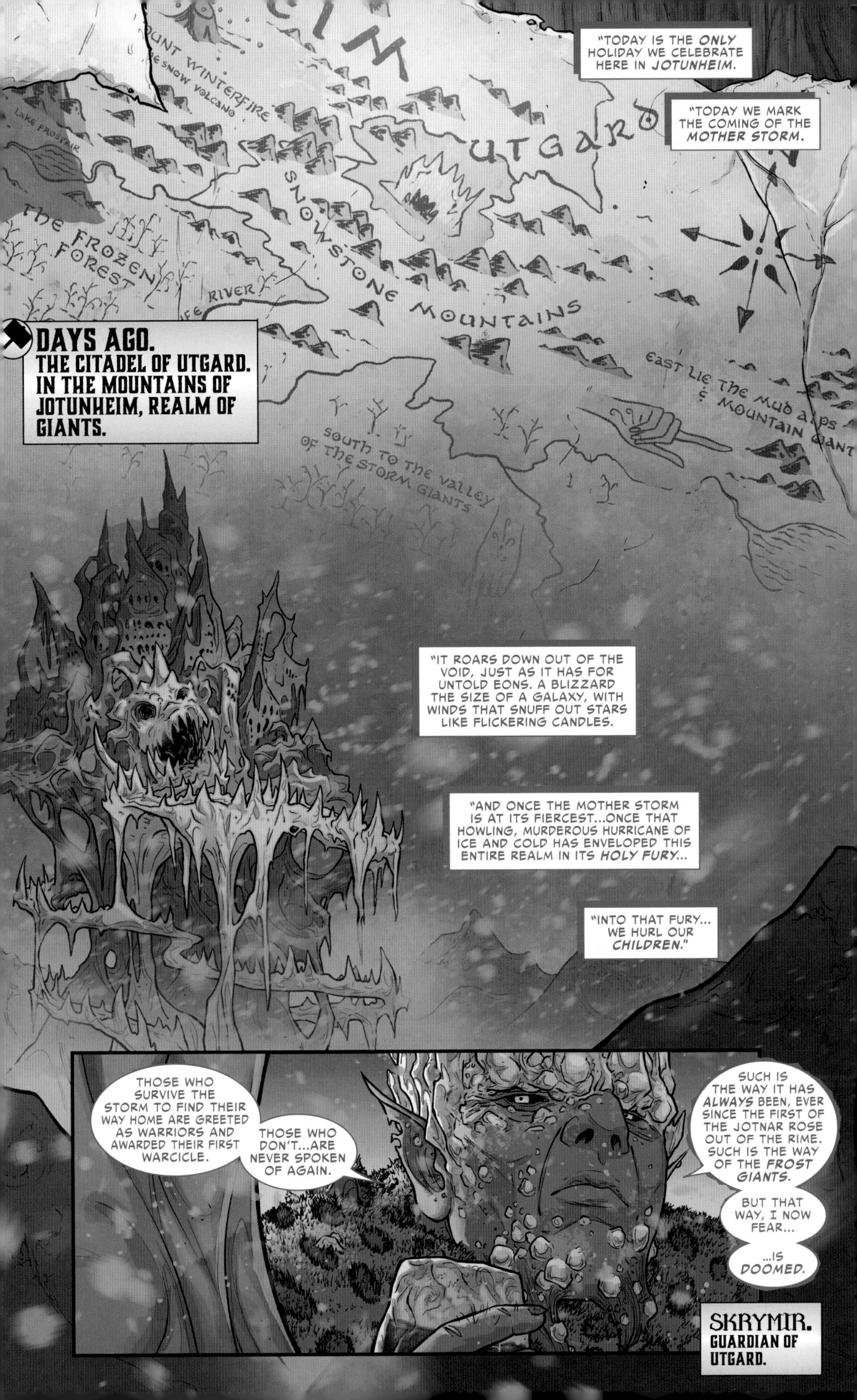
"TODAY IS THE ONLY HOLIDAY WE CELEBRATE HERE IN JOTUNHEIM.
"TODAY WE MARK THE COMING OF THE MOTHER STORM.
MOUNT WINTERFIRE
THE SNOW VOLCANO
LAKE PROSTAIR
UTGARD
SNOWSTONE MOUNTAINS
THE FROZEN FOREST
RIVER
DAYS AGO. THE CITADEL OF UTGARD. IN THE MOUNTAINS OF JOTUNHEIM, REALM OF GIANTS.
EAST LIE THE MUD ALPS & MOUNTAIN GIANT
SOUTH TO THE VALLEY OF THE STORM GIANTS
"IT ROARS DOWN OUT OF THE VOID, JUST AS IT HAS FOR UNTOLD EONS. A BLIZZARD THE SIZE OF A GALAXY, WITH WINDS THAT SNUFF OUT STARS LIKE FLICKERING CANDLES.
"AND ONCE THE MOTHER STORM IS AT ITS FIERCEST...ONCE THAT HOWLING, MURDEROUS HURRICANE OF ICE AND COLD HAS ENVELOPED THIS ENTIRE REALM IN ITS HOLY FURY...
"INTO THAT FURY... WE HURL OUR CHILDREN."
THOSE WHO SURVIVE THE STORM TO FIND THEIR WAY HOME ARE GREETED AS WARRIORS AND AWARDED THEIR FIRST WARCICLE.
THOSE WHO DON'T...ARE NEVER SPOKEN OF AGAIN.
SUCH IS THE WAY IT HAS ALWAYS BEEN, EVER SINCE THE FIRST OF THE JOTNAR ROSE OUT OF THE RIME. SUCH IS THE WAY OF THE FROST GIANTS.
BUT THAT WAY, I NOW FEAR...
...IS DOOMED.
SKRYMIR. GUARDIAN OF UTGARD.

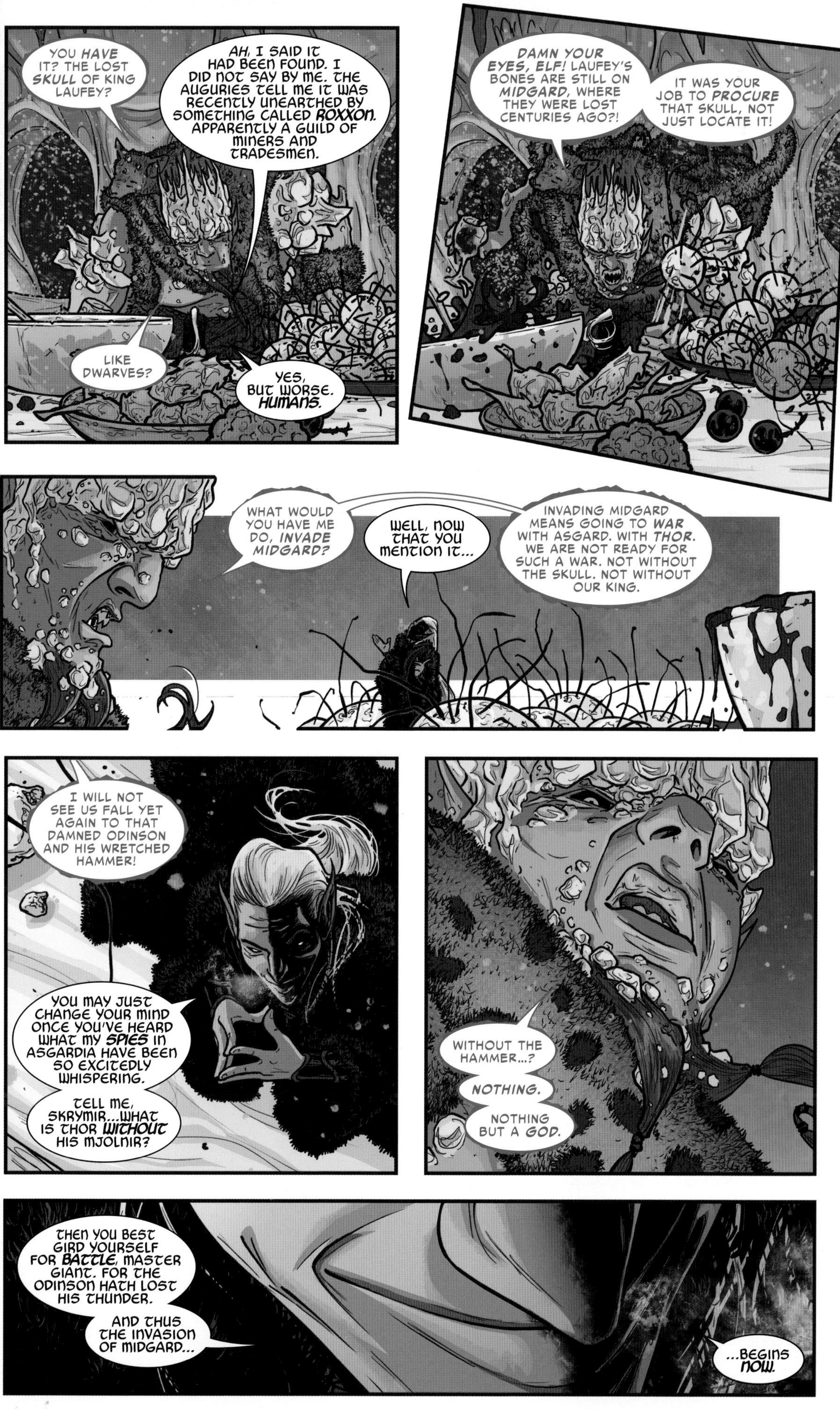
YOU HAVE IT? THE LOST SKULL OF KING LAUFEY?
AH, I SAID IT HAD BEEN FOUND. I DID NOT SAY BY ME. THE AUGURIES TELL ME IT WAS RECENTLY UNEARTHED BY SOMETHING CALLED ROXXON. APPARENTLY A GUILD OF MINERS AND TRADESMEN.
LIKE DWARVES?
YES, BUT WORSE. HUMANS.
DAMN YOUR EYES, ELF! LAUFEY'S BONES ARE STILL ON MIDGARD, WHERE THEY WERE LOST CENTURIES AGO?!
IT WAS YOUR JOB TO PROCURE THAT SKULL, NOT JUST LOCATE IT!
WHAT WOULD YOU HAVE ME DO, INVADE MIDGARD?
WELL, NOW THAT YOU MENTION IT...
INVADING MIDGARD MEANS GOING TO WAR WITH ASGARD. WITH THOR. WE ARE NOT READY FOR SUCH A WAR. NOT WITHOUT THE SKULL. NOT WITHOUT OUR KING.
I WILL NOT SEE US FALL YET AGAIN TO THAT DAMNED ODINSON AND HIS WRETCHED HAMMER!
YOU MAY JUST CHANGE YOUR MIND ONCE YOU'VE HEARD WHAT MY SPIES IN ASGARDIA HAVE BEEN SO EXCITEDLY WHISPERING.
TELL ME, SKRYMIR...WHAT IS THOR WITHOUT HIS MJOLNIR?
WITHOUT THE HAMMER...?
NOTHING.
NOTHING BUT A GOD.
THEN YOU BEST GIRD YOURSELF FOR BATTLE, MASTER GIANT. FOR THE ODINSON HATH LOST HIS THUNDER.
AND THUS THE INVASION OF MIDGARD...
...BEGINS NOW.

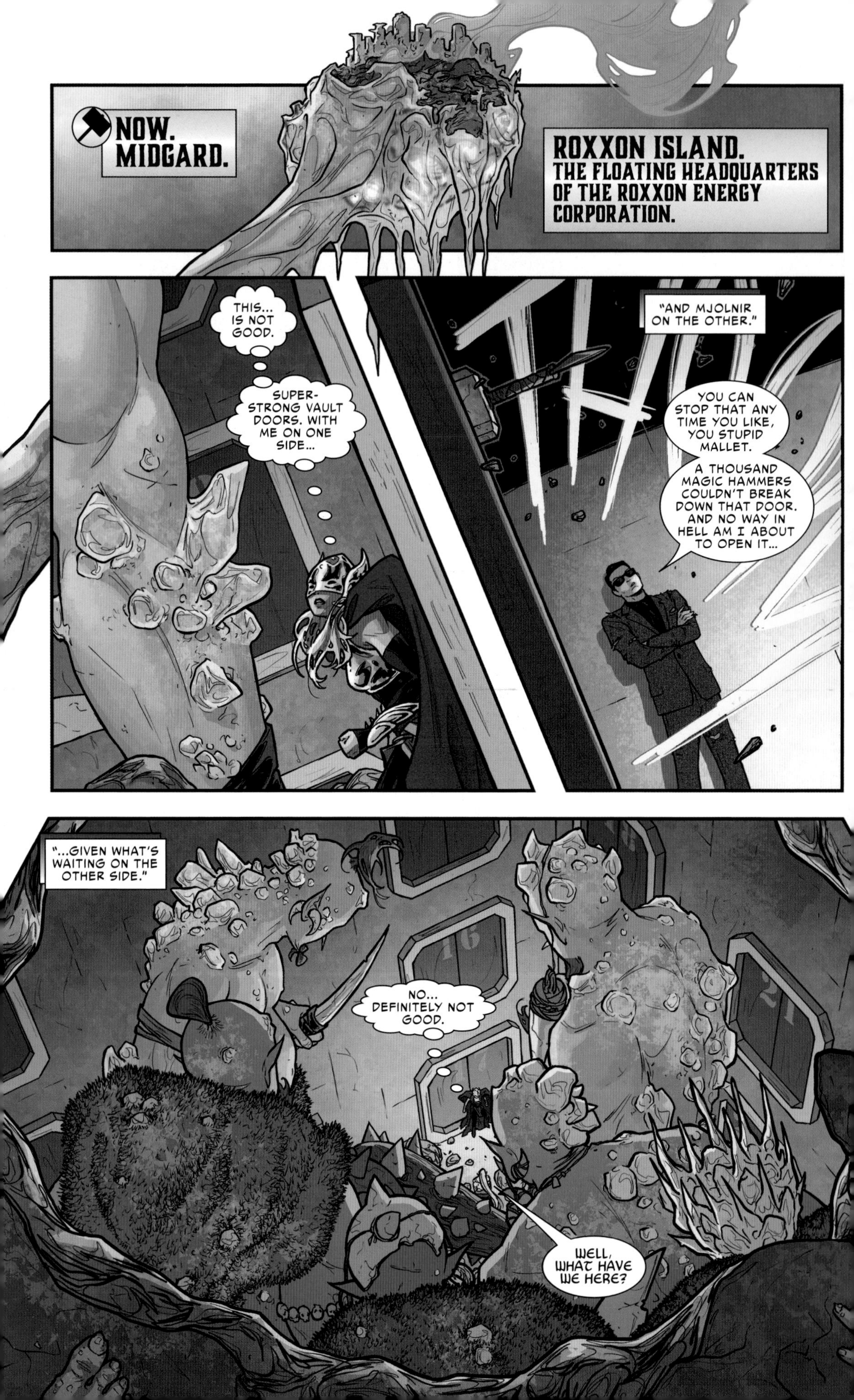
NOW.
MIDGARD.
ROXXON ISLAND.
THE FLOATING HEADQUARTERS OF THE ROXXON ENERGY CORPORATION.
THIS... IS NOT GOOD.
SUPER-STRONG VAULT DOORS. WITH ME ON ONE SIDE...
"AND MJOLNIR ON THE OTHER."
YOU CAN STOP THAT ANY TIME YOU LIKE, YOU STUPID MALLET.
A THOUSAND MAGIC HAMMERS COULDN'T BREAK DOWN THAT DOOR. AND NO WAY IN HELL AM I ABOUT TO OPEN IT...
"...GIVEN WHAT'S WAITING ON THE OTHER SIDE."
NO... DEFINITELY NOT GOOD.
WELL, WHAT HAVE WE HERE?

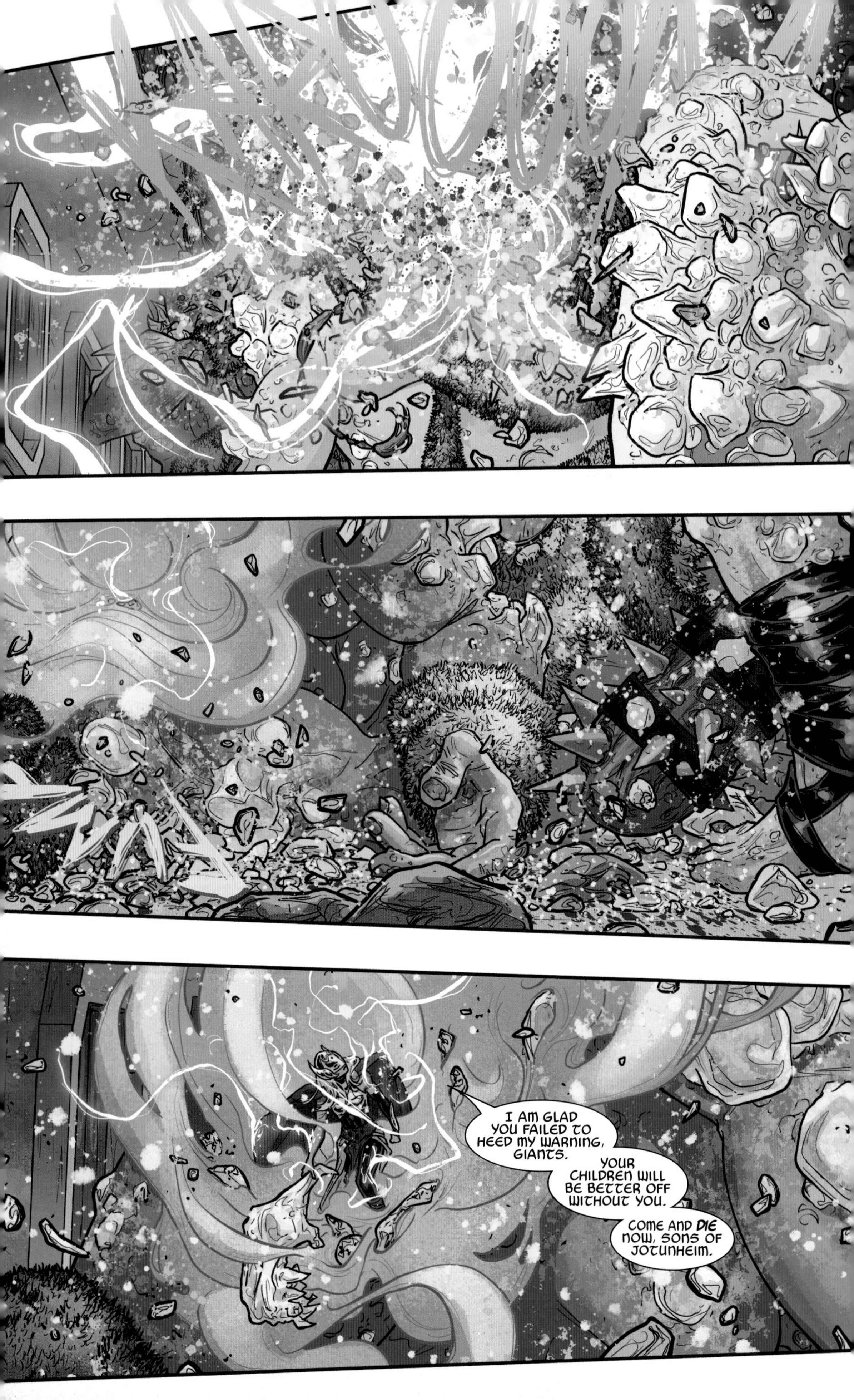
I AM GLAD YOU FAILED TO HEED MY WARNING, GIANTS.
YOUR CHILDREN WILL BE BETTER OFF WITHOUT YOU.
COME AND **DIE** NOW, SONS OF JOTUNHEIM.

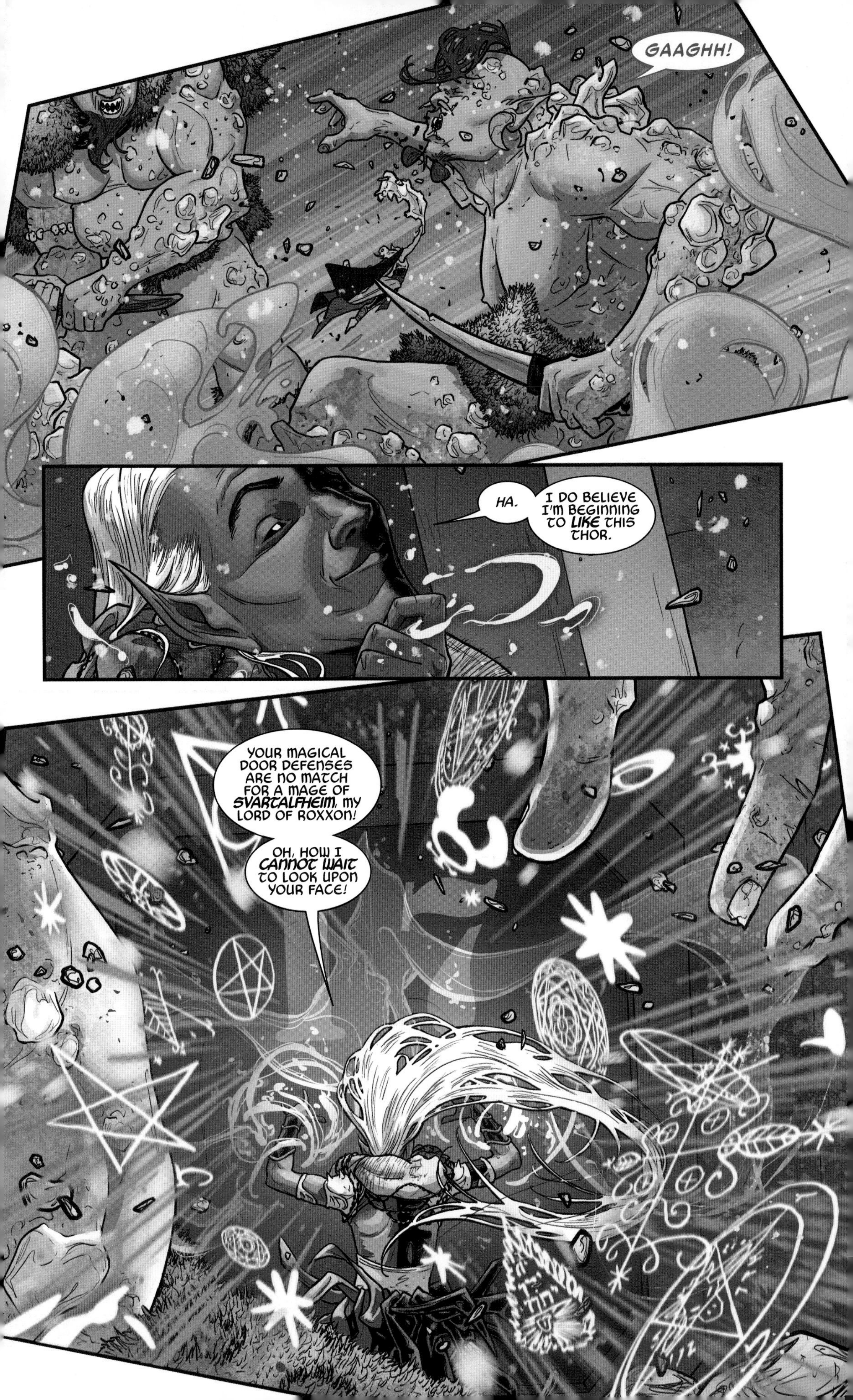
GAAGHH!
HA.
I DO BELIEVE I'M BEGINNING TO LIKE THIS THOR.
YOUR MAGICAL DOOR DEFENSES ARE NO MATCH FOR A MAGE OF SVARTALFHEIM, MY LORD OF ROXXON!
OH, HOW I CANNOT WAIT TO LOOK UPON YOUR FACE!

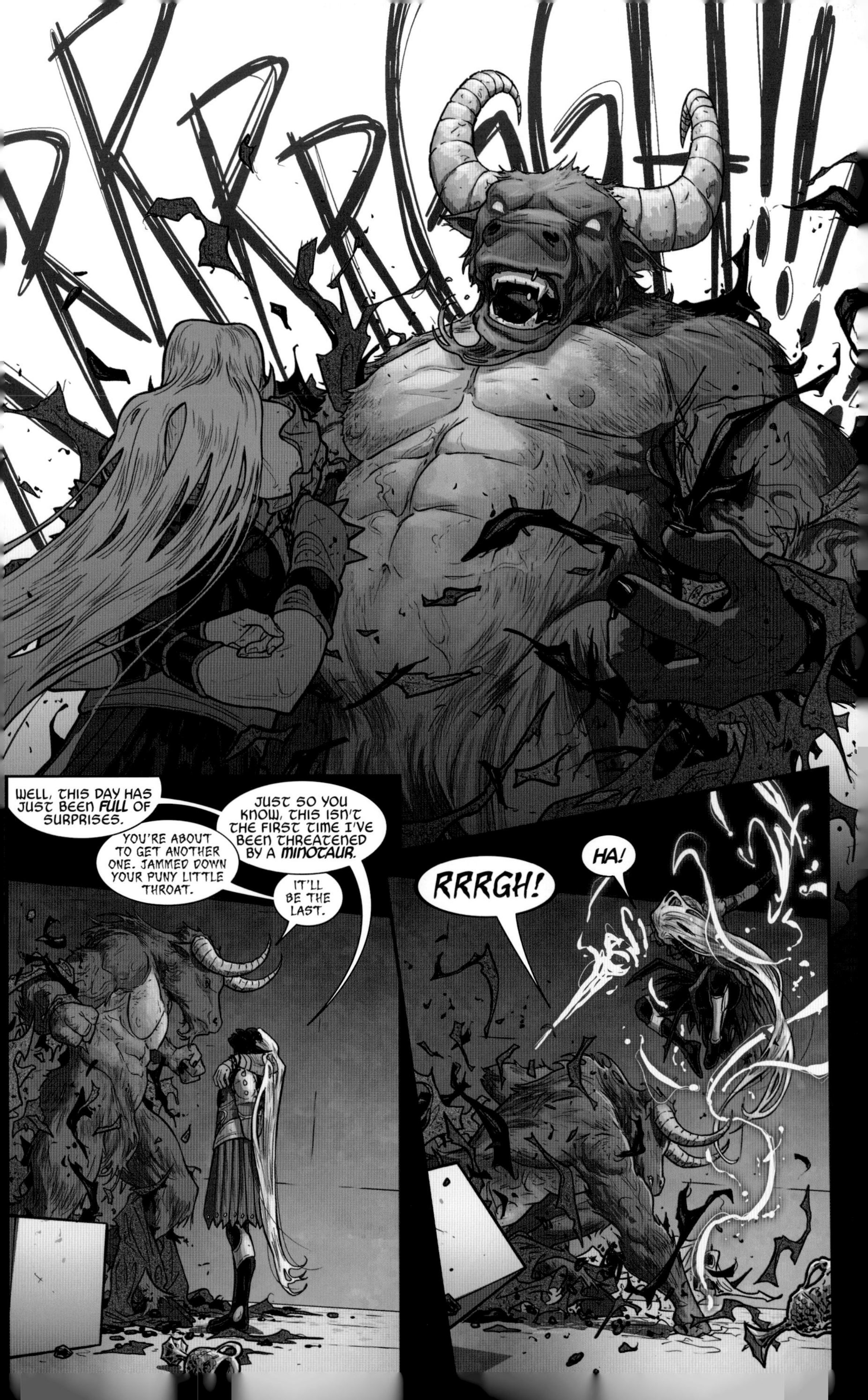
WELL, THIS DAY HAS JUST BEEN **FULL** OF SURPRISES.
JUST SO YOU KNOW, THIS ISN'T THE FIRST TIME I'VE BEEN THREATENED BY A ***MINOTAUR***.
YOU'RE ABOUT TO GET ANOTHER ONE. JAMMED DOWN YOUR PUNY LITTLE THROAT.
IT'LL BE THE LAST.
RRRGH!
HA!

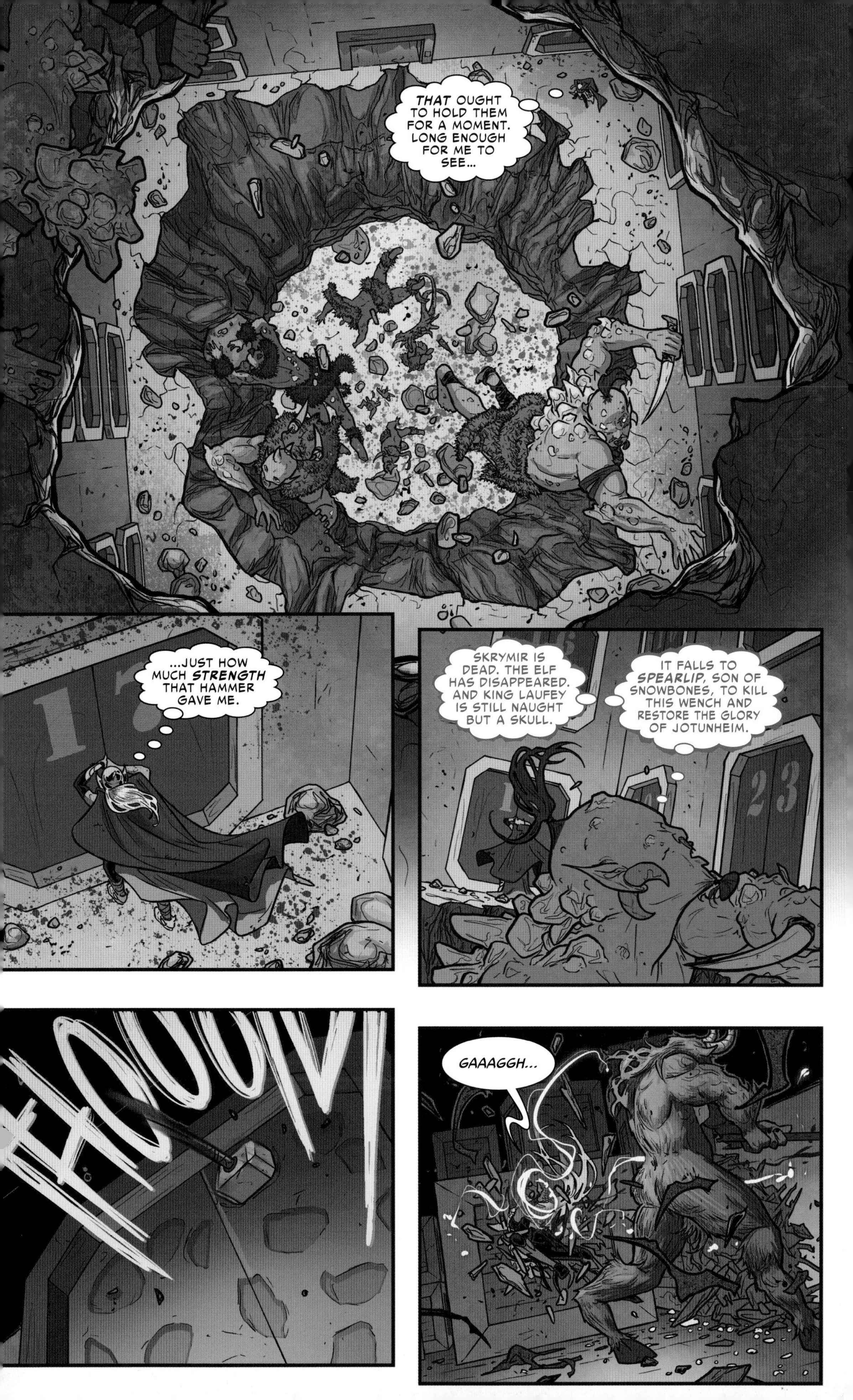
THAT OUGHT TO HOLD THEM FOR A MOMENT. LONG ENOUGH FOR ME TO SEE...
...JUST HOW MUCH STRENGTH THAT HAMMER GAVE ME.
SKRYMIR IS DEAD. THE ELF HAS DISAPPEARED. AND KING LAUFEY IS STILL NAUGHT BUT A SKULL.
IT FALLS TO SPEARLIP, SON OF SNOWBONES, TO KILL THIS WENCH AND RESTORE THE GLORY OF JOTUNHEIM.
THOOOM
GAAAGGH...

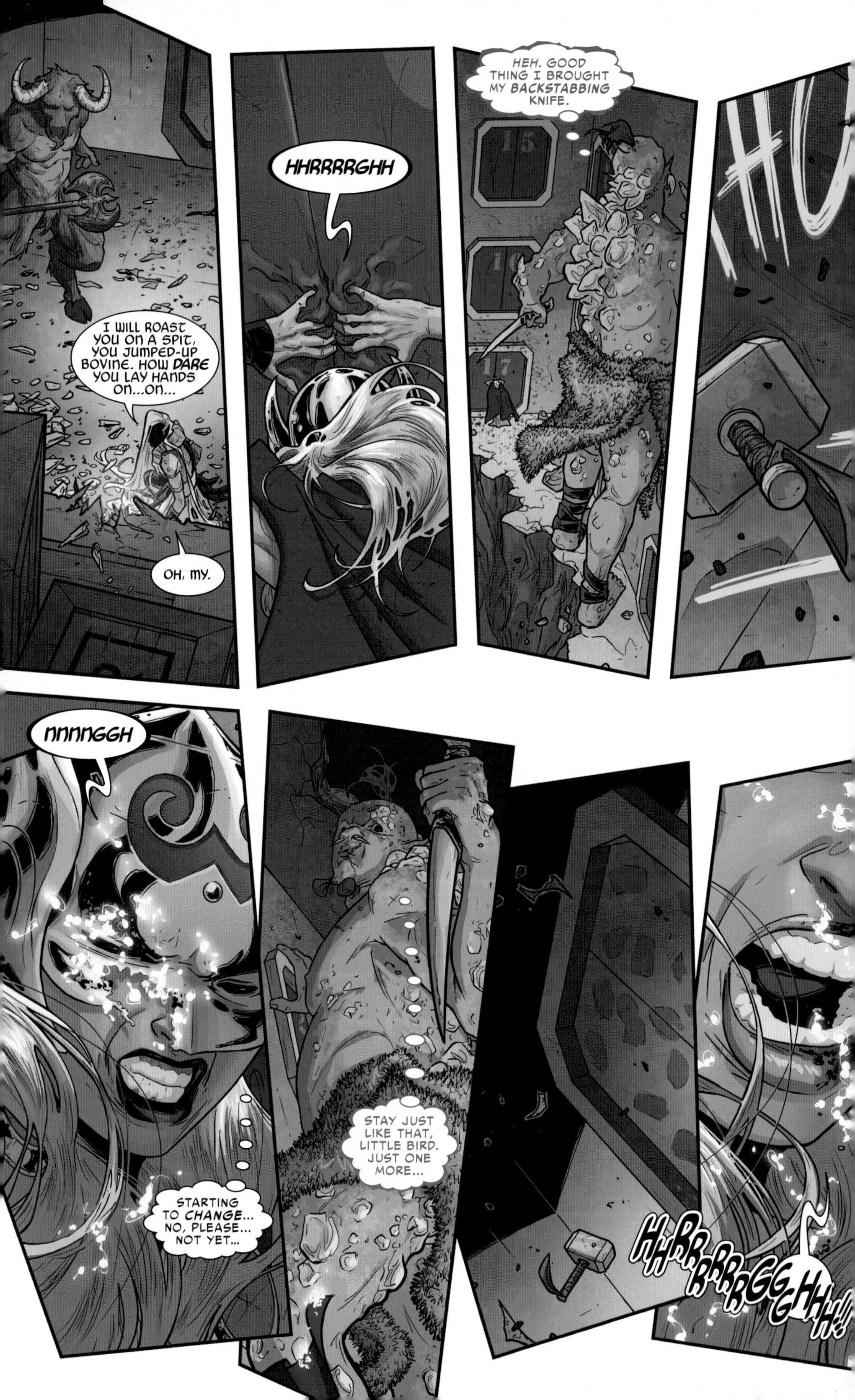
I WILL ROAST YOU ON A SPIT, YOU JUMPED-UP BOVINE. HOW DARE YOU LAY HANDS ON...ON...
OH, MY.
HHRRRRGHH
HEH. GOOD THING I BROUGHT MY BACKSTABBING KNIFE.
15
16
17
NNNNGGH
STARTING TO CHANGE... NO, PLEASE... NOT YET...
STAY JUST LIKE THAT, LITTLE BIRD. JUST ONE MORE...
HHRRRRRRGGHHH!

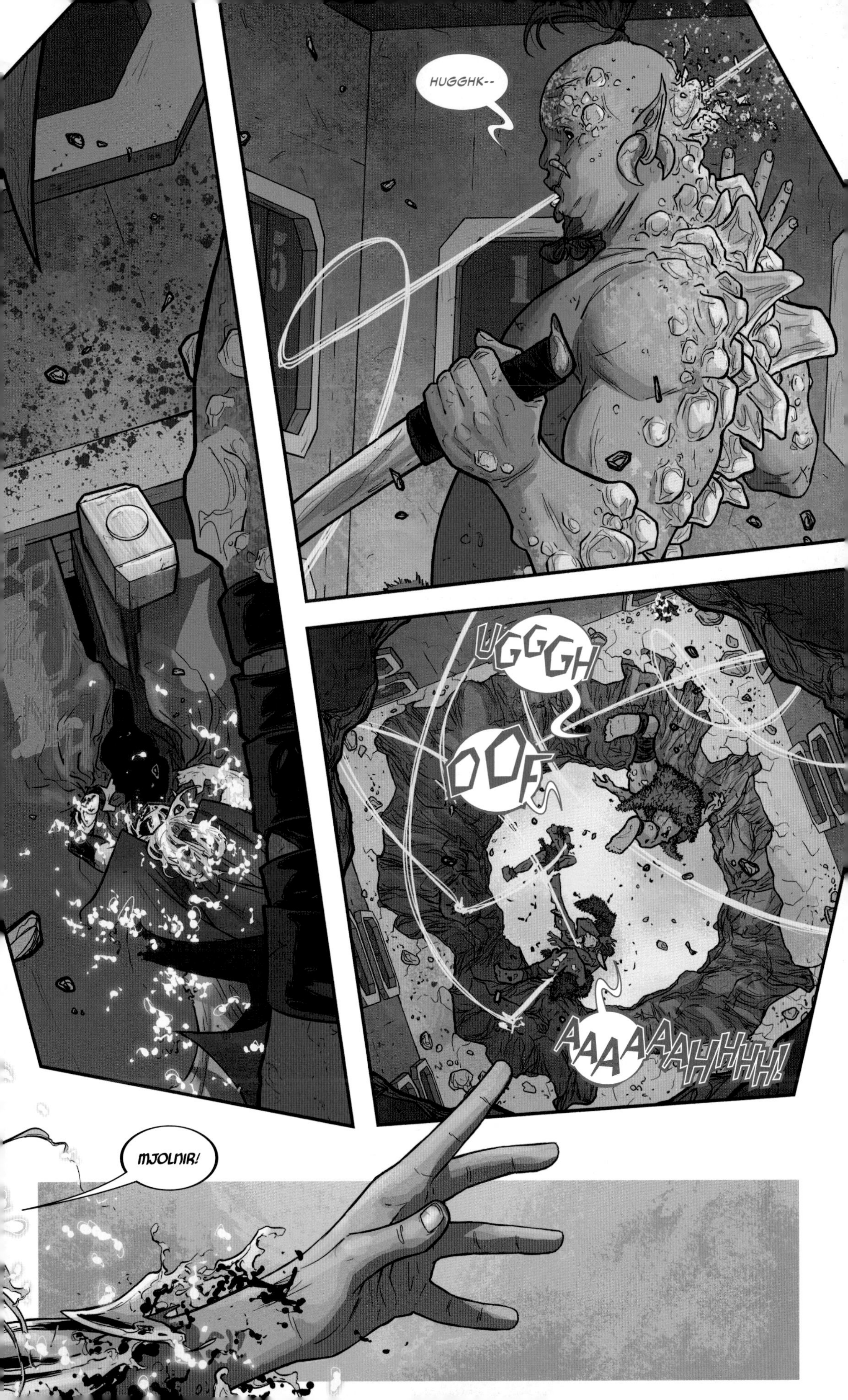
HUGGHK--
UGGGH
OOF
AAAAAAHHHHH!
MJOLNIR!

ALL THIS FIGHTING? ALL THIS DEATH? AND ALL FOR *WHAT?*

BONES. BONES AND PRIDE, THAT IS ALL I SEE. AND I BELIEVE I HAVE SEEN QUITE ENOUGH OF BOTH.

WAIT...WHAT ARE YOU DOING... STAY AWAY FROM THE SKULL--

IF ONLY I COULD SMASH YOUR PRIDE AS EASILY. SHALL WE *TRY?*

YOU...HAVE JUST *DOOMED* THIS REALM, YOU FOOLISH FEMALE! IF YOU THOUGHT THIS WAS WAR *BEFORE,* YOU WERE WRONG.

WAR IS WHAT WILL HAPPEN *NOW,* ONCE THE FROST GIANTS LEARN WHAT YOU HAVE DONE.

THEY WILL RAGE AND RAZE UNTIL THE SUN GROWS COLD. THEY WILL SEND MIDGARD BACK TO THE *ICE AGE.*

TELL ME, "GODDESS OF THUNDER"...IS THAT A WAR YOU'RE PREPARED TO FIGHT?

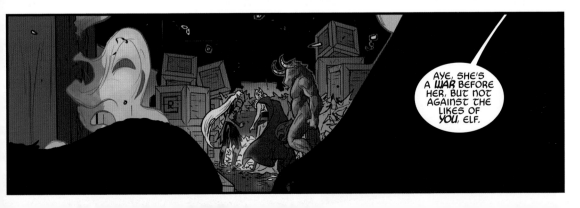

AYE, SHE'S A *WAR* BEFORE HER, BUT NOT AGAINST THE LIKES OF *YOU,* ELF.

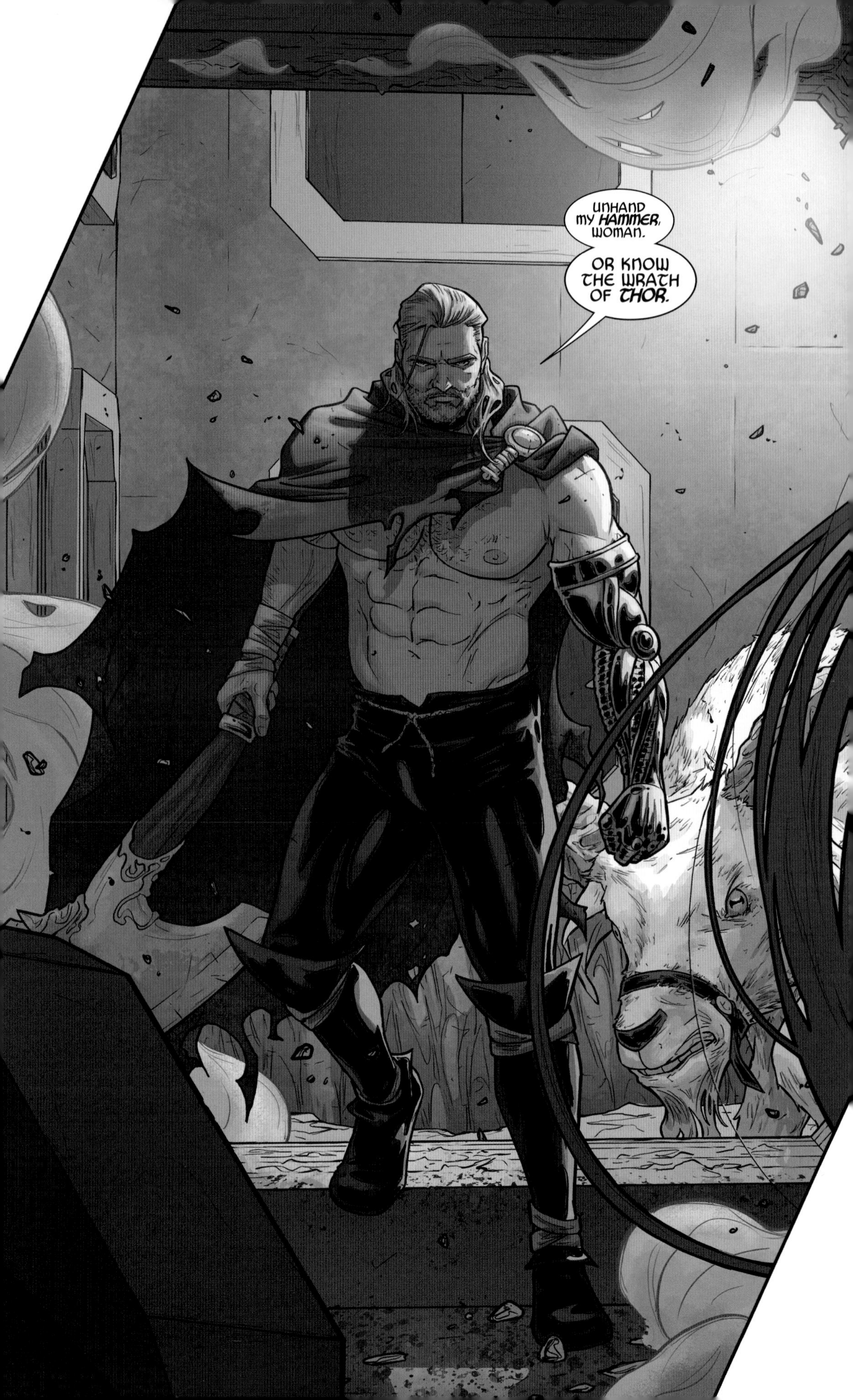
UNHAND my HAMMER, WOMAN.
OR KNOW THE WRATH OF THOR.

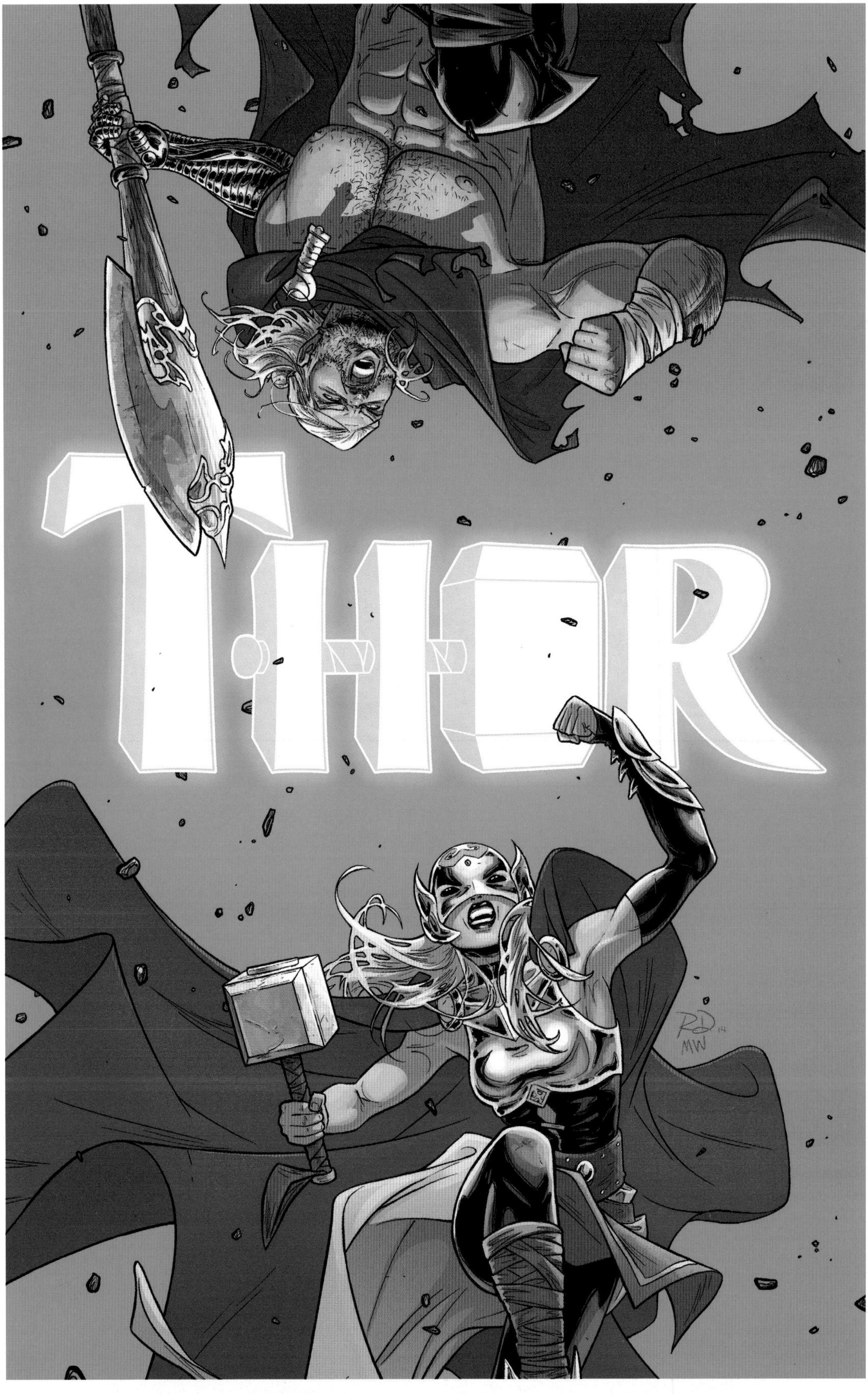
THOR

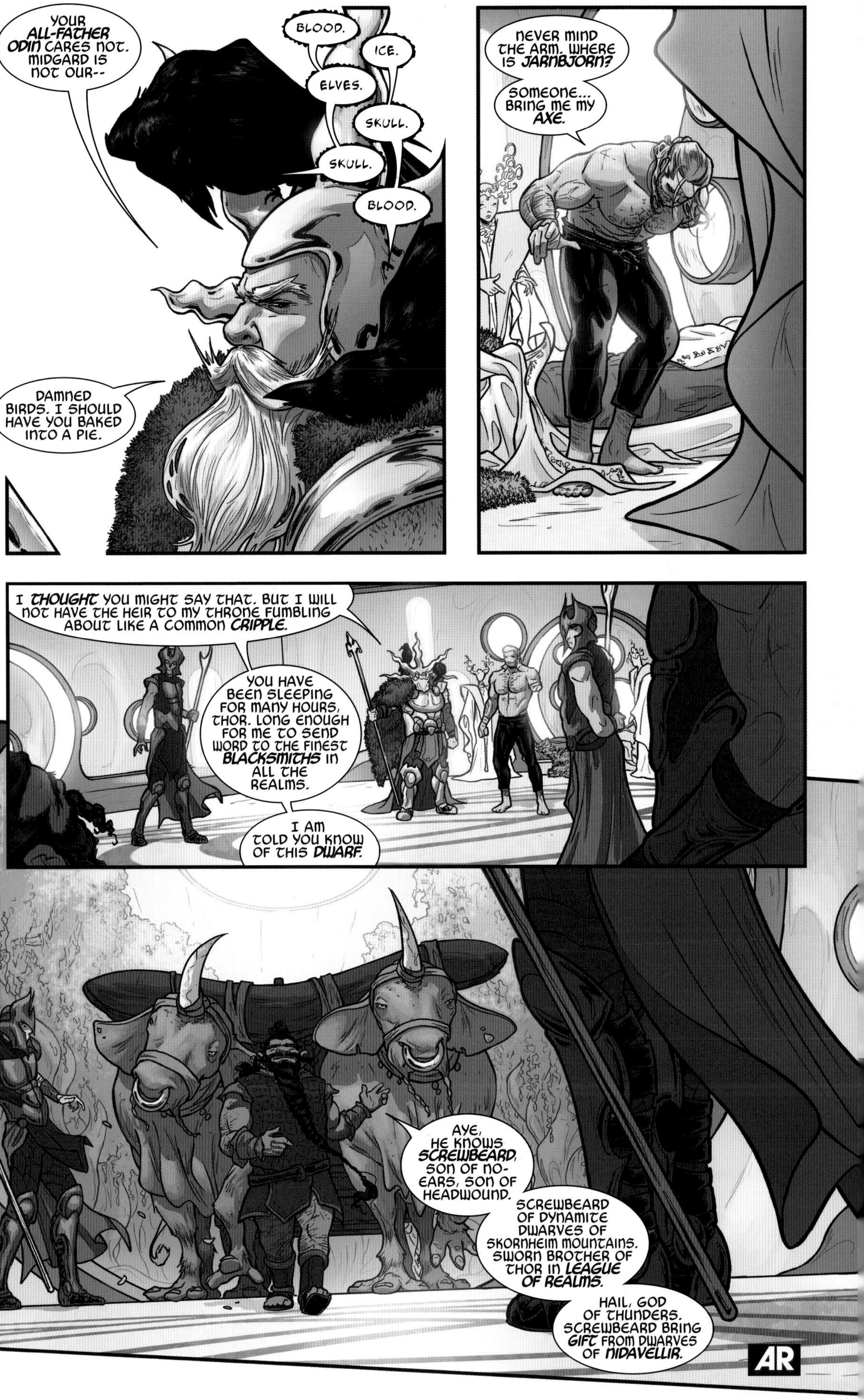
YOUR ALL-FATHER ODIN CARES NOT. MIDGARD IS NOT OUR--
BLOOD.
ICE.
ELVES.
SKULL.
SKULL.
BLOOD.
DAMNED BIRDS. I SHOULD HAVE YOU BAKED INTO A PIE.
NEVER MIND THE ARM. WHERE IS JARNBJORN?
SOMEONE... BRING ME MY AXE.
I THOUGHT YOU MIGHT SAY THAT. BUT I WILL NOT HAVE THE HEIR TO MY THRONE FUMBLING ABOUT LIKE A COMMON CRIPPLE.
YOU HAVE BEEN SLEEPING FOR MANY HOURS, THOR. LONG ENOUGH FOR ME TO SEND WORD TO THE FINEST BLACKSMITHS IN ALL THE REALMS.
I AM TOLD YOU KNOW OF THIS DWARF.
AYE, HE KNOWS SCREWBEARD, SON OF NO-EARS, SON OF HEADWOUND.
SCREWBEARD OF DYNAMITE DWARVES OF SKORNHEIM MOUNTAINS. SWORN BROTHER OF THOR IN LEAGUE OF REALMS.
HAIL, GOD OF THUNDERS. SCREWBEARD BRING GIFT FROM DWARVES OF NIDAVELLIR.
AR

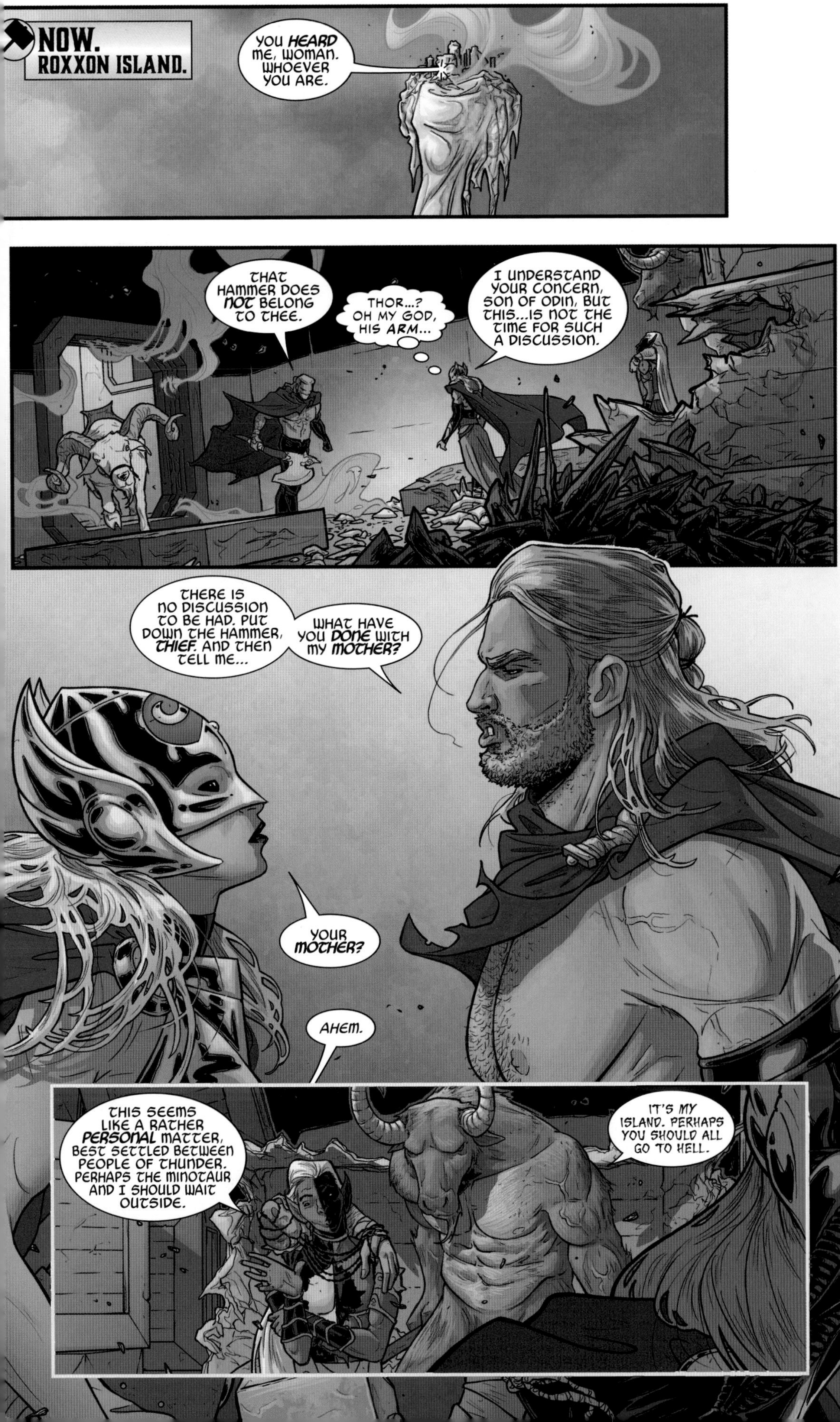

NOW. ROXXON ISLAND.
YOU HEARD ME, WOMAN. WHOEVER YOU ARE.
THAT HAMMER DOES NOT BELONG TO THEE.
THOR...? OH MY GOD, HIS ARM...
I UNDERSTAND YOUR CONCERN, SON OF ODIN, BUT THIS...IS NOT THE TIME FOR SUCH A DISCUSSION.
THERE IS NO DISCUSSION TO BE HAD. PUT DOWN THE HAMMER, THIEF. AND THEN TELL ME...
WHAT HAVE YOU DONE WITH MY MOTHER?
YOUR MOTHER?
AHEM.
THIS SEEMS LIKE A RATHER PERSONAL MATTER, BEST SETTLED BETWEEN PEOPLE OF THUNDER. PERHAPS THE MINOTAUR AND I SHOULD WAIT OUTSIDE.
IT'S MY ISLAND. PERHAPS YOU SHOULD ALL GO TO HELL.

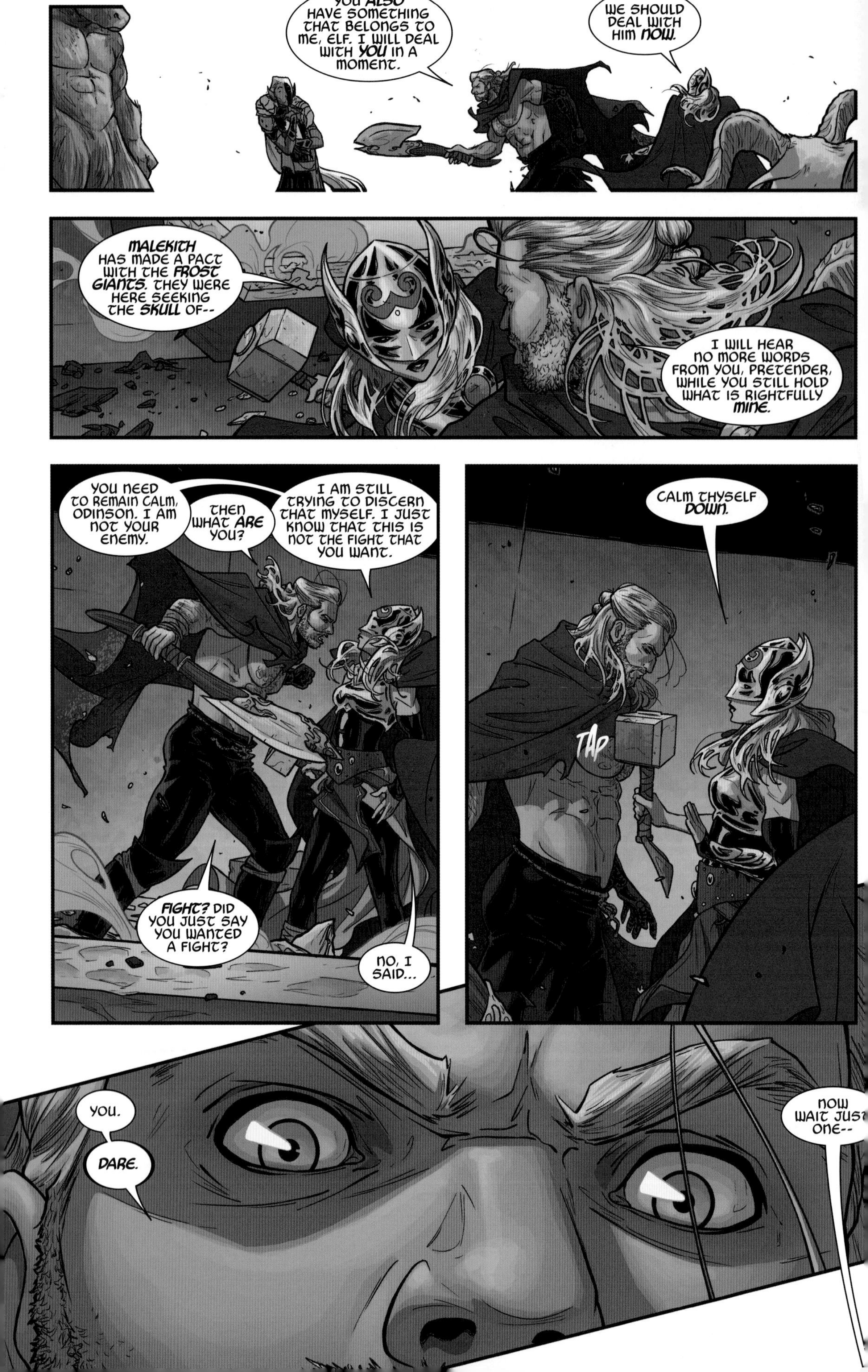
YOU ALSO HAVE SOMETHING THAT BELONGS TO ME, ELF. I WILL DEAL WITH YOU IN A MOMENT.
WE SHOULD DEAL WITH HIM NOW.
MALEKITH HAS MADE A PACT WITH THE FROST GIANTS. THEY WERE HERE SEEKING THE SKULL OF--
I WILL HEAR NO MORE WORDS FROM YOU, PRETENDER, WHILE YOU STILL HOLD WHAT IS RIGHTFULLY MINE.
YOU NEED TO REMAIN CALM, ODINSON. I AM NOT YOUR ENEMY.
THEN WHAT ARE YOU?
I AM STILL TRYING TO DISCERN THAT MYSELF. I JUST KNOW THAT THIS IS NOT THE FIGHT THAT YOU WANT.
FIGHT? DID YOU JUST SAY YOU WANTED A FIGHT?
NO, I SAID...
CALM THYSELF DOWN.
TAP
YOU.
DARE.
NOW WAIT JUST ONE--

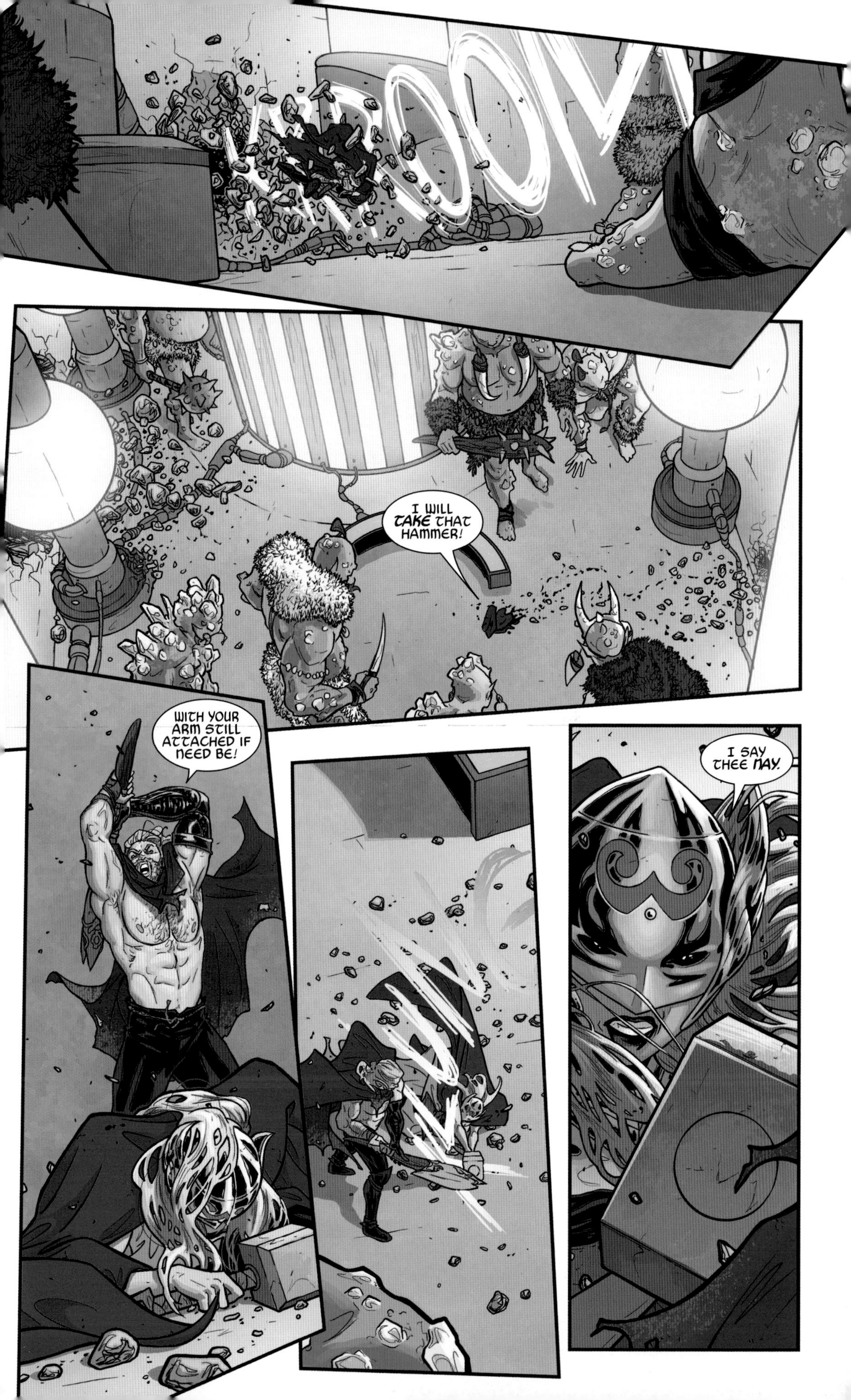
KRDOOM
I WILL TAKE THAT HAMMER!
WITH YOUR ARM STILL ATTACHED IF NEED BE!
I SAY THEE NAY.

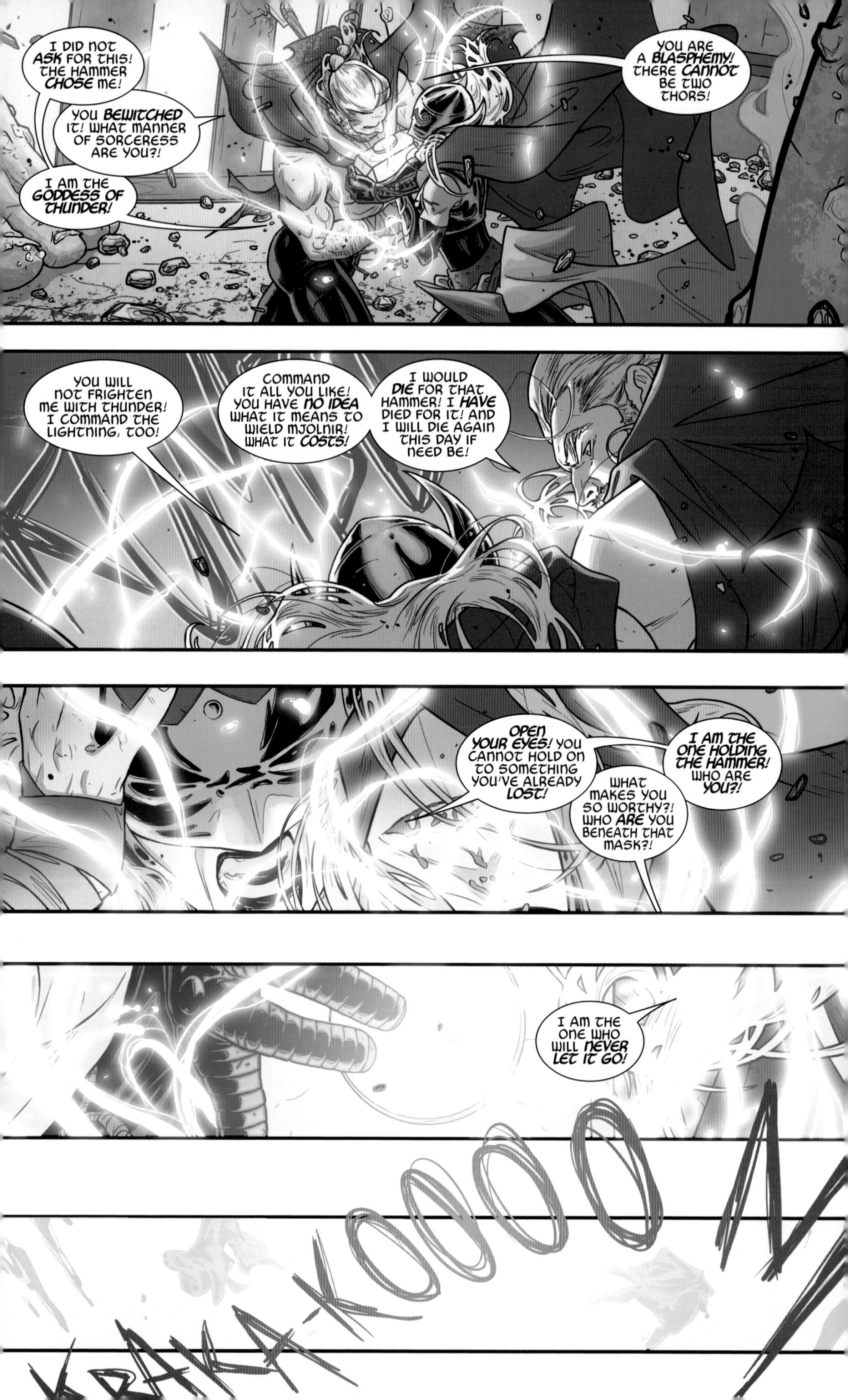
I DID NOT ASK FOR THIS! THE HAMMER CHOSE ME!
YOU ARE A BLASPHEMY! THERE CANNOT BE TWO THORS!
YOU BEWITCHED IT! WHAT MANNER OF SORCERESS ARE YOU?!
I AM THE GODDESS OF THUNDER!
YOU WILL NOT FRIGHTEN ME WITH THUNDER! I COMMAND THE LIGHTNING, TOO!
COMMAND IT ALL YOU LIKE! YOU HAVE NO IDEA WHAT IT MEANS TO WIELD MJOLNIR! WHAT IT COSTS!
I WOULD DIE FOR THAT HAMMER! I HAVE DIED FOR IT! AND I WILL DIE AGAIN THIS DAY IF NEED BE!
OPEN YOUR EYES! YOU CANNOT HOLD ON TO SOMETHING YOU'VE ALREADY LOST!
I AM THE ONE HOLDING THE HAMMER! WHO ARE YOU?!
WHAT MAKES YOU SO WORTHY?! WHO ARE YOU BENEATH THAT MASK?!
I AM THE ONE WHO WILL NEVER LET IT GO!
KRAKA-KOOOOOM

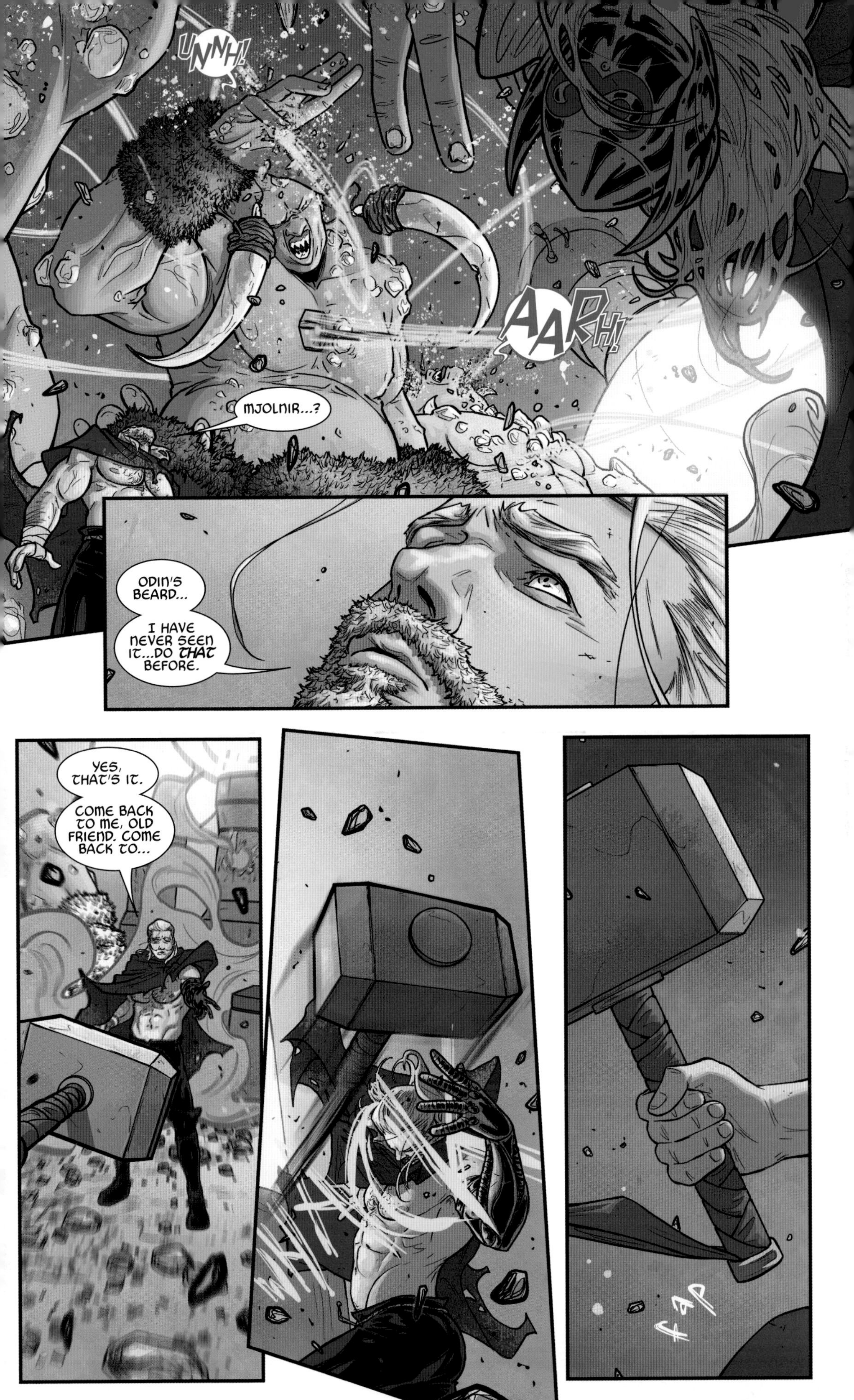
UNNH!
AARH!
MJOLNIR...?
ODIN'S BEARD...
I HAVE NEVER SEEN IT...DO *THAT* BEFORE.
YES, THAT'S IT.
COME BACK TO ME, OLD FRIEND. COME BACK TO...
TAP

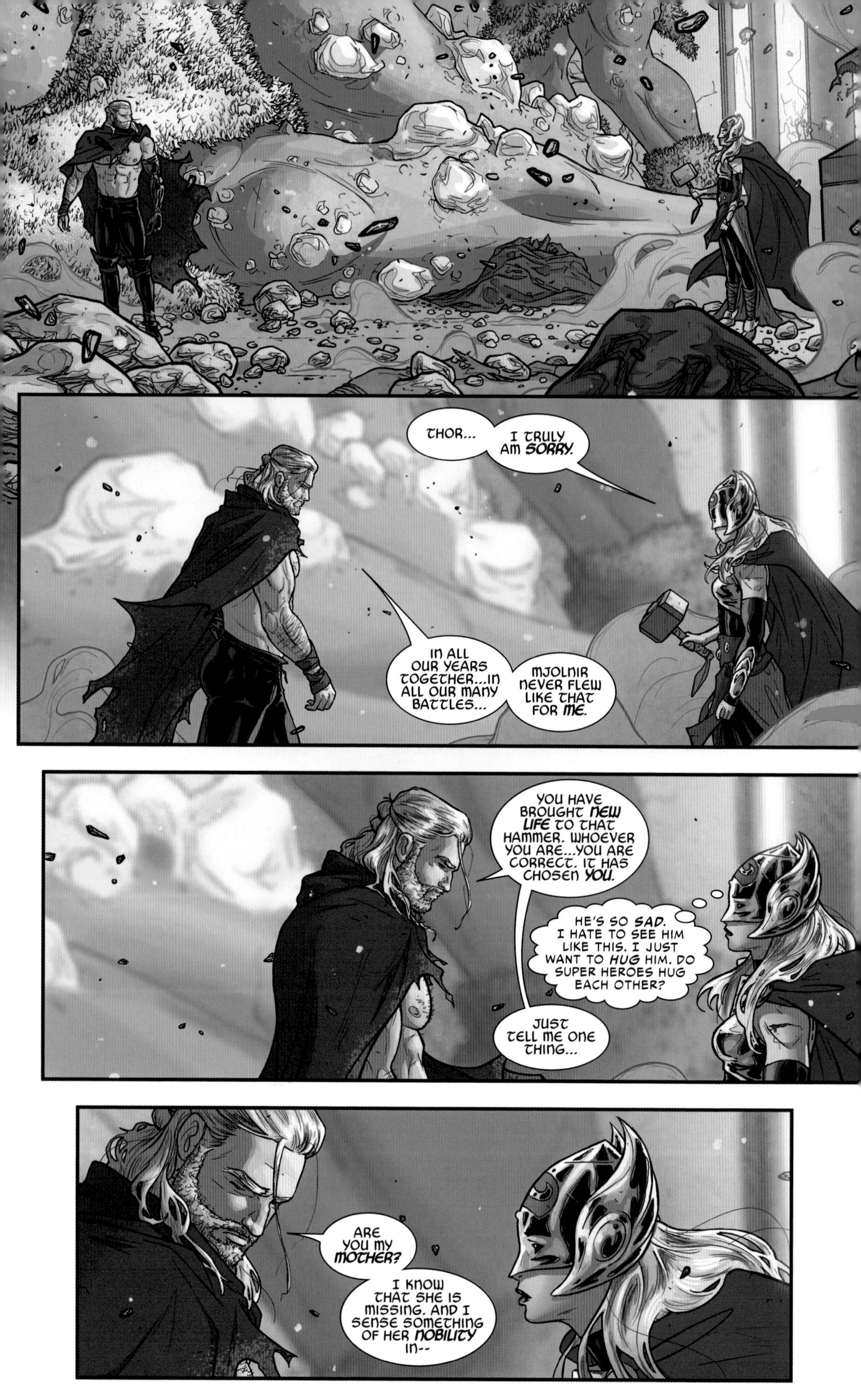
THOR...
I TRULY AM SORRY.
IN ALL OUR YEARS TOGETHER...IN ALL OUR MANY BATTLES...
MJOLNIR NEVER FLEW LIKE THAT FOR ME.
YOU HAVE BROUGHT NEW LIFE TO THAT HAMMER. WHOEVER YOU ARE...YOU ARE CORRECT. IT HAS CHOSEN YOU.
HE'S SO SAD. I HATE TO SEE HIM LIKE THIS. I JUST WANT TO HUG HIM. DO SUPER HEROES HUG EACH OTHER?
JUST TELL ME ONE THING...
ARE YOU MY MOTHER?
I KNOW THAT SHE IS MISSING. AND I SENSE SOMETHING OF HER NOBILITY IN--

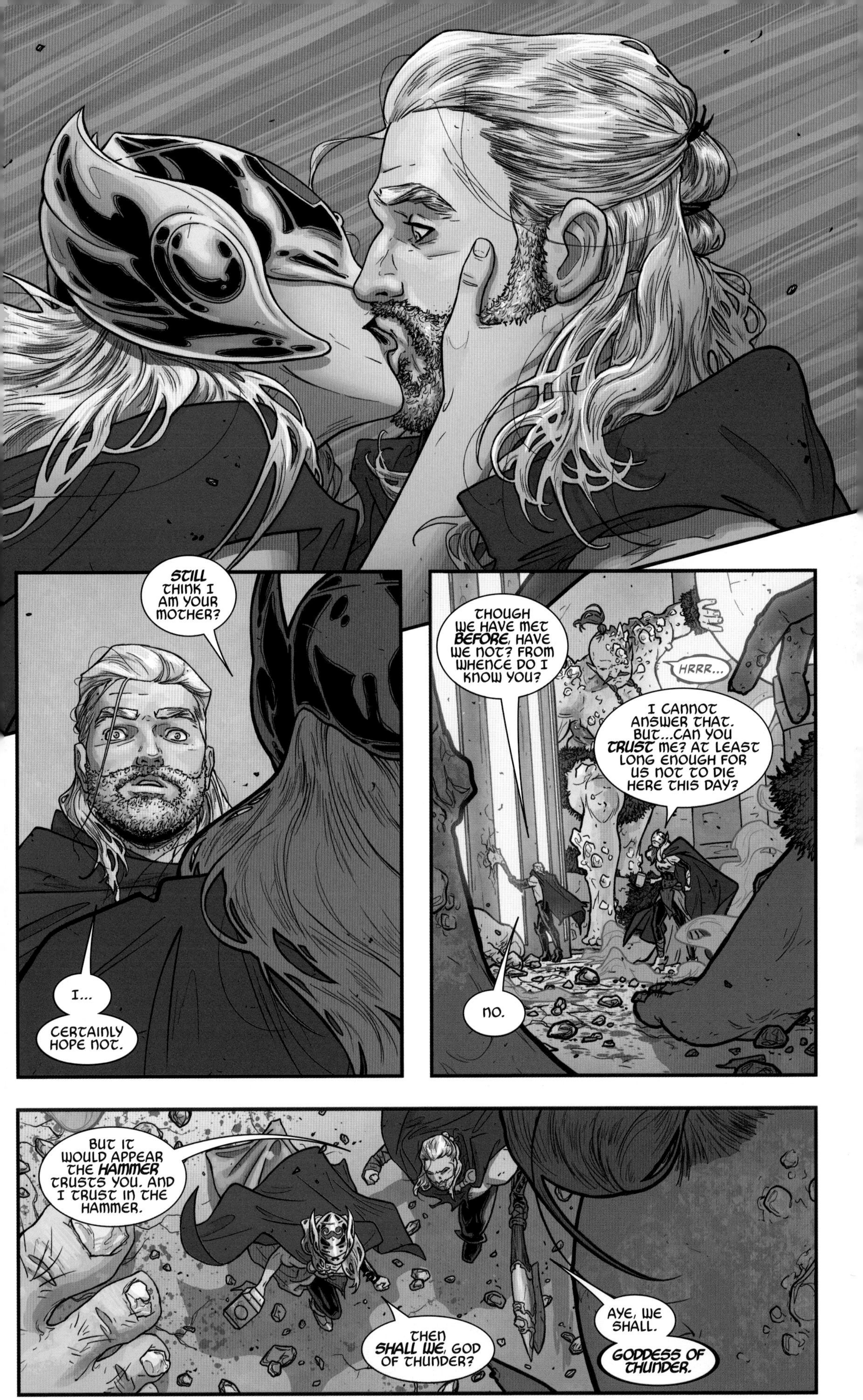

STILL THINK I AM YOUR MOTHER?
I...
CERTAINLY HOPE NOT.
THOUGH WE HAVE MET BEFORE, HAVE WE NOT? FROM WHENCE DO I KNOW YOU?
HRRR...
I CANNOT ANSWER THAT. BUT...CAN YOU TRUST ME? AT LEAST LONG ENOUGH FOR US NOT TO DIE HERE THIS DAY?
NO.
BUT IT WOULD APPEAR THE HAMMER TRUSTS YOU. AND I TRUST IN THE HAMMER.
THEN SHALL WE, GOD OF THUNDER?
AYE, WE SHALL.
GODDESS OF THUNDER.

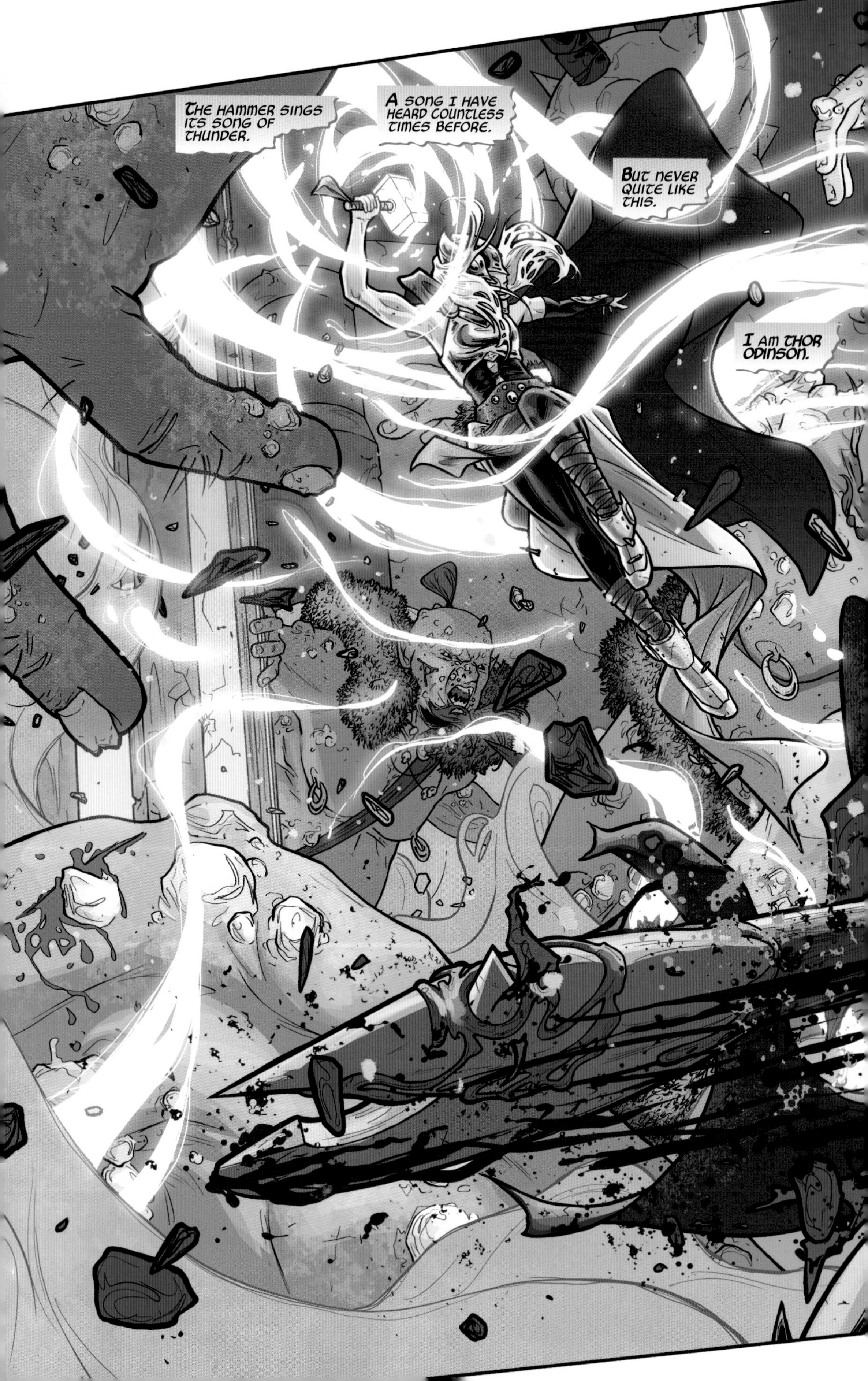

THE HAMMER SINGS ITS SONG OF THUNDER.
A SONG I HAVE HEARD COUNTLESS TIMES BEFORE.
BUT NEVER QUITE LIKE THIS.
I AM THOR ODINSON.

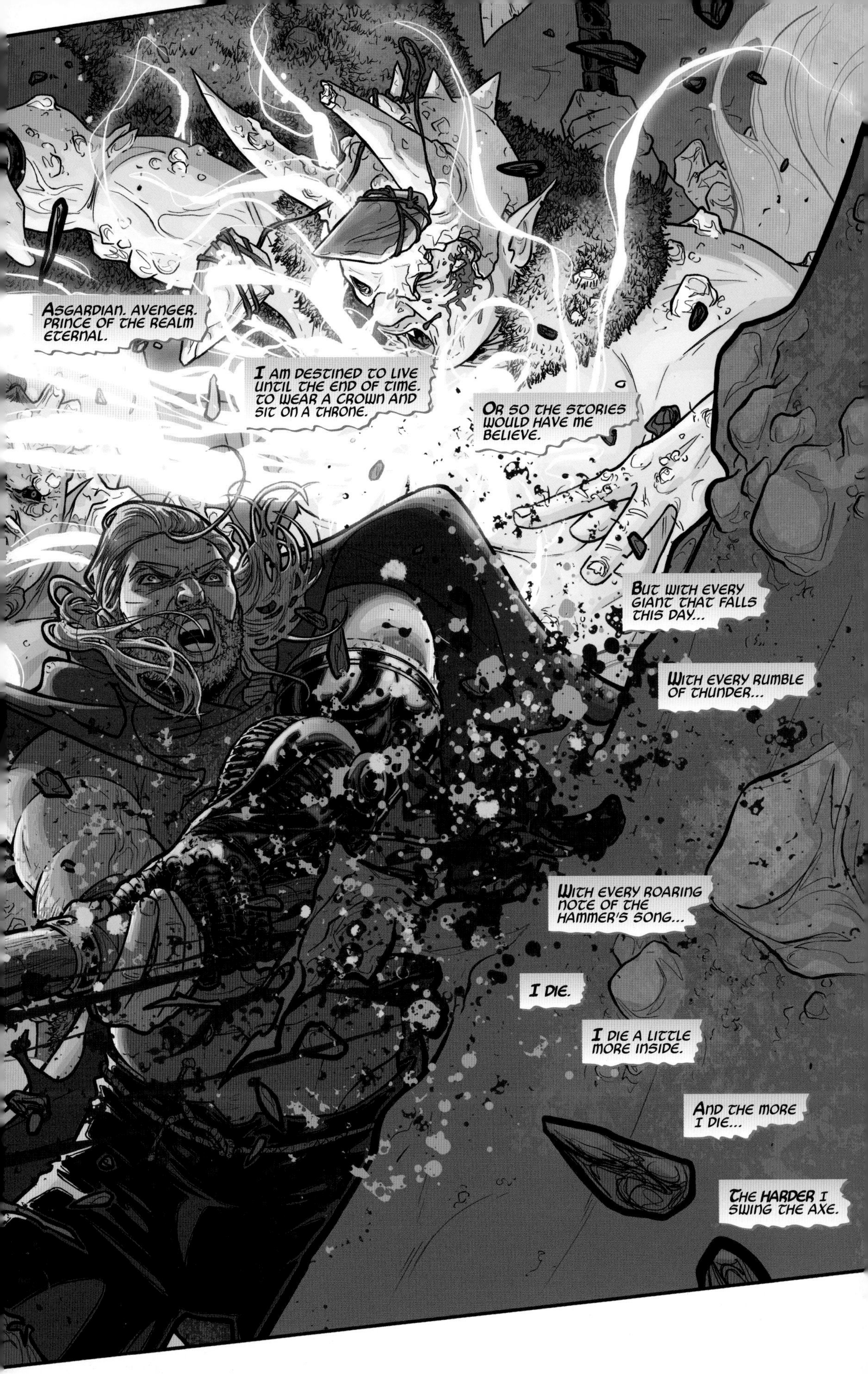
ASGARDIAN. AVENGER. PRINCE OF THE REALM ETERNAL.
I AM DESTINED TO LIVE UNTIL THE END OF TIME. TO WEAR A CROWN AND SIT ON A THRONE.
OR SO THE STORIES WOULD HAVE ME BELIEVE.
BUT WITH EVERY GIANT THAT FALLS THIS DAY...
WITH EVERY RUMBLE OF THUNDER...
WITH EVERY ROARING NOTE OF THE HAMMER'S SONG...
I DIE.
I DIE A LITTLE MORE INSIDE.
AND THE MORE I DIE...
THE HARDER I SWING THE AXE.

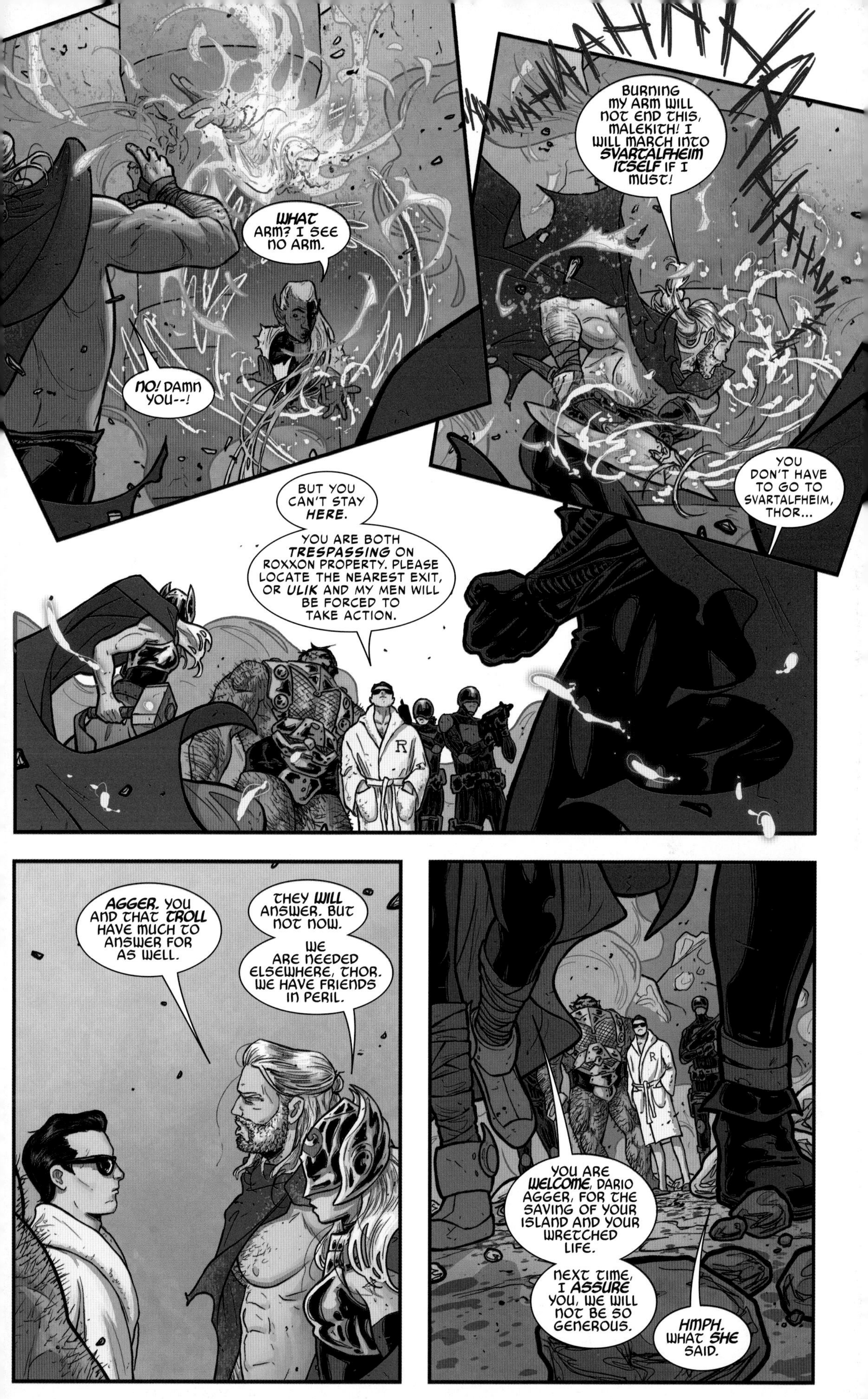
WHAT ARM? I SEE NO ARM.
NO! DAMN YOU--!
HAHAHAHAHAHAHAHAHA
BURNING MY ARM WILL NOT END THIS, MALEKITH! I WILL MARCH INTO SVARTALFHEIM ITSELF IF I MUST!
YOU DON'T HAVE TO GO TO SVARTALFHEIM, THOR...
BUT YOU CAN'T STAY HERE.
YOU ARE BOTH TRESPASSING ON ROXXON PROPERTY. PLEASE LOCATE THE NEAREST EXIT, OR ULIK AND MY MEN WILL BE FORCED TO TAKE ACTION.
R
AGGER. YOU AND THAT TROLL HAVE MUCH TO ANSWER FOR AS WELL.
THEY WILL ANSWER. BUT NOT NOW.
WE ARE NEEDED ELSEWHERE, THOR. WE HAVE FRIENDS IN PERIL.
R
YOU ARE WELCOME, DARIO AGGER, FOR THE SAVING OF YOUR ISLAND AND YOUR WRETCHED LIFE.
NEXT TIME, I ASSURE YOU, WE WILL NOT BE SO GENEROUS.
HMPH. WHAT SHE SAID.

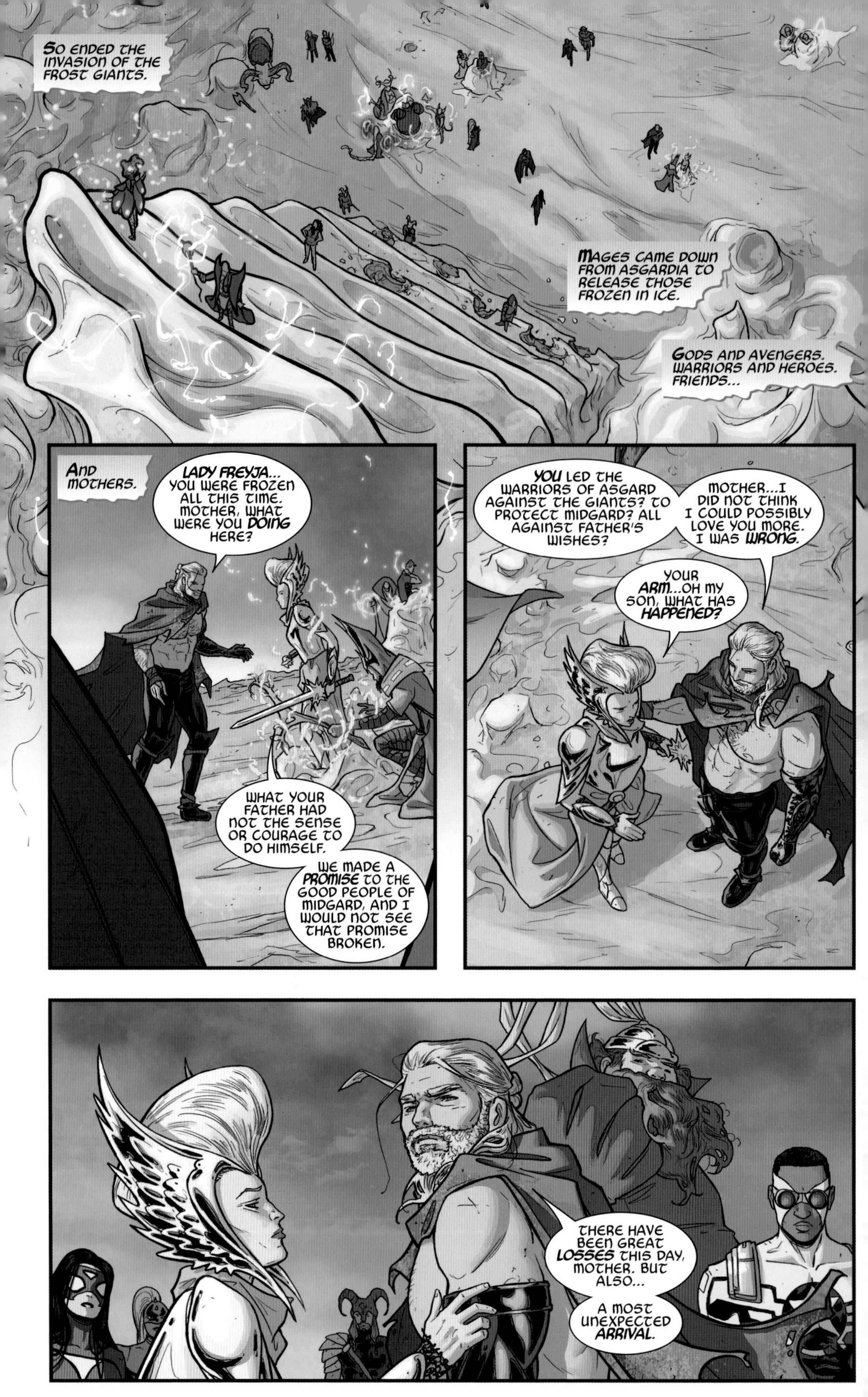
So ended the invasion of the frost giants.
Mages came down from Asgardia to release those frozen in ice.
Gods and Avengers. Warriors and heroes. Friends...
And mothers.
Lady Freyja... you were frozen all this time. Mother, what were you doing here?
What your father had not the sense or courage to do himself.
We made a promise to the good people of Midgard, and I would not see that promise broken.
You led the warriors of Asgard against the giants? To protect Midgard? All against father's wishes?
Mother...I did not think I could possibly love you more. I was wrong.
Your arm...oh my son, what has happened?
There have been great losses this day, mother. But also...
A most unexpected arrival.

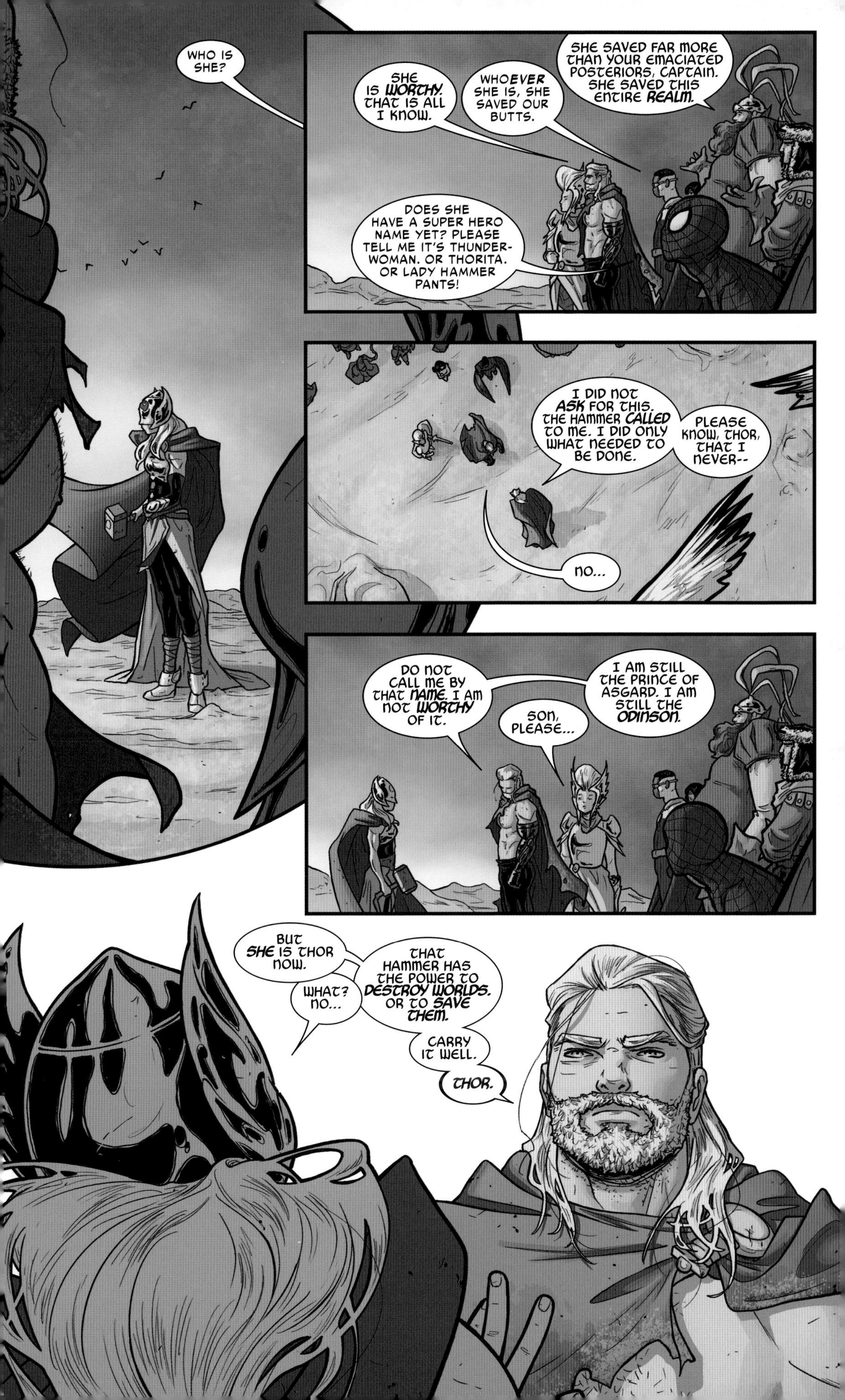
WHO IS SHE?
SHE IS WORTHY. THAT IS ALL I KNOW.
WHOEVER SHE IS, SHE SAVED OUR BUTTS.
SHE SAVED FAR MORE THAN YOUR EMACIATED POSTERIORS, CAPTAIN. SHE SAVED THIS ENTIRE REALM.
DOES SHE HAVE A SUPER HERO NAME YET? PLEASE TELL ME IT'S THUNDER-WOMAN. OR THORITA. OR LADY HAMMER PANTS!
I DID NOT ASK FOR THIS. THE HAMMER CALLED TO ME. I DID ONLY WHAT NEEDED TO BE DONE.
PLEASE KNOW, THOR, THAT I NEVER--
NO...
DO NOT CALL ME BY THAT NAME. I AM NOT WORTHY OF IT.
I AM STILL THE PRINCE OF ASGARD. I AM STILL THE ODINSON.
SON, PLEASE...
BUT SHE IS THOR NOW.
WHAT? NO...
THAT HAMMER HAS THE POWER TO DESTROY WORLDS. OR TO SAVE THEM.
CARRY IT WELL.
THOR.

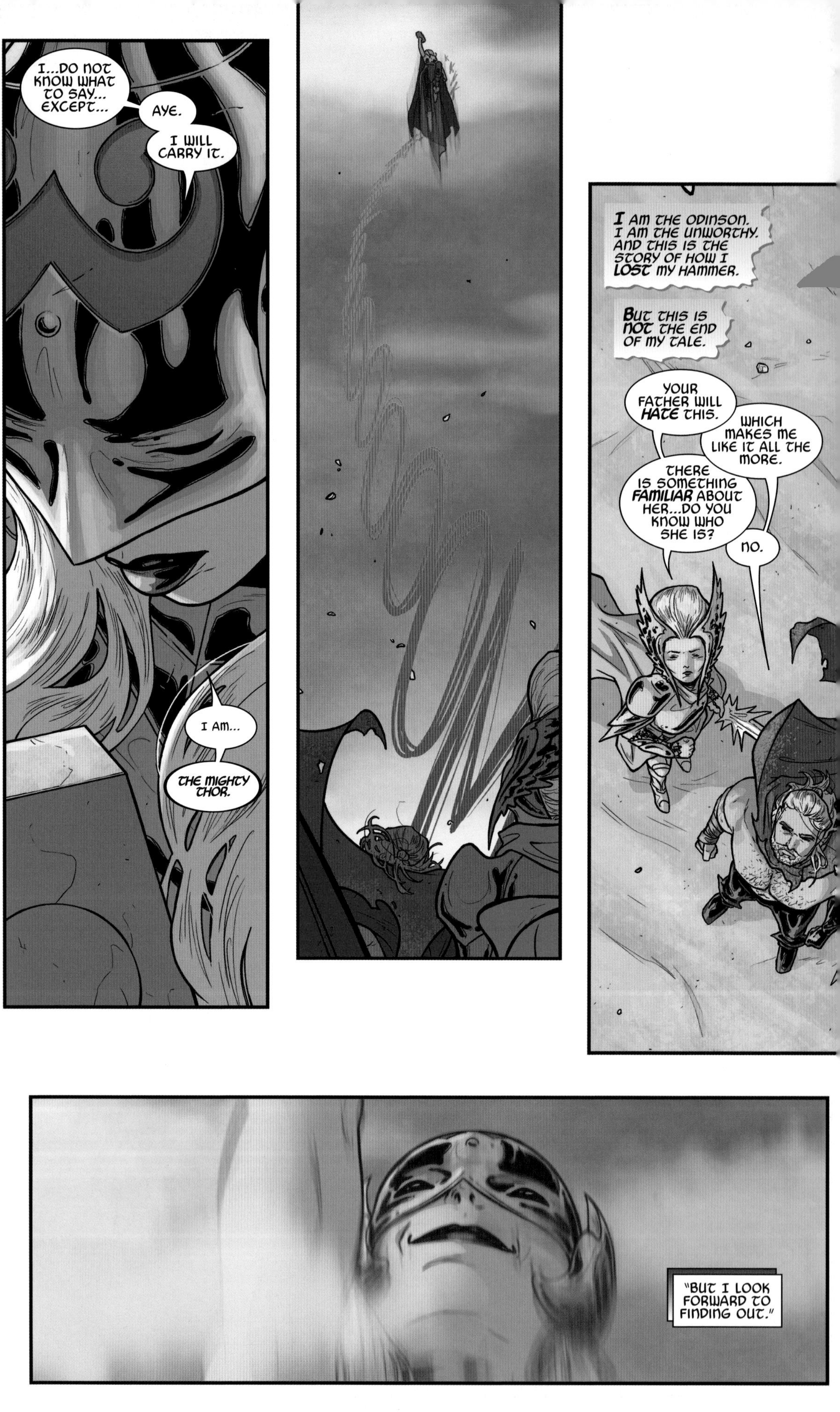

I...DO NOT KNOW WHAT TO SAY... EXCEPT...
AYE.
I WILL CARRY IT.
I AM...
THE MIGHTY THOR.
I AM THE ODINSON. I AM THE UNWORTHY. AND THIS IS THE STORY OF HOW I LOST MY HAMMER.
BUT THIS IS NOT THE END OF MY TALE.
YOUR FATHER WILL HATE THIS.
WHICH MAKES ME LIKE IT ALL THE MORE.
THERE IS SOMETHING FAMILIAR ABOUT HER...DO YOU KNOW WHO SHE IS?
NO.
"BUT I LOOK FORWARD TO FINDING OUT."

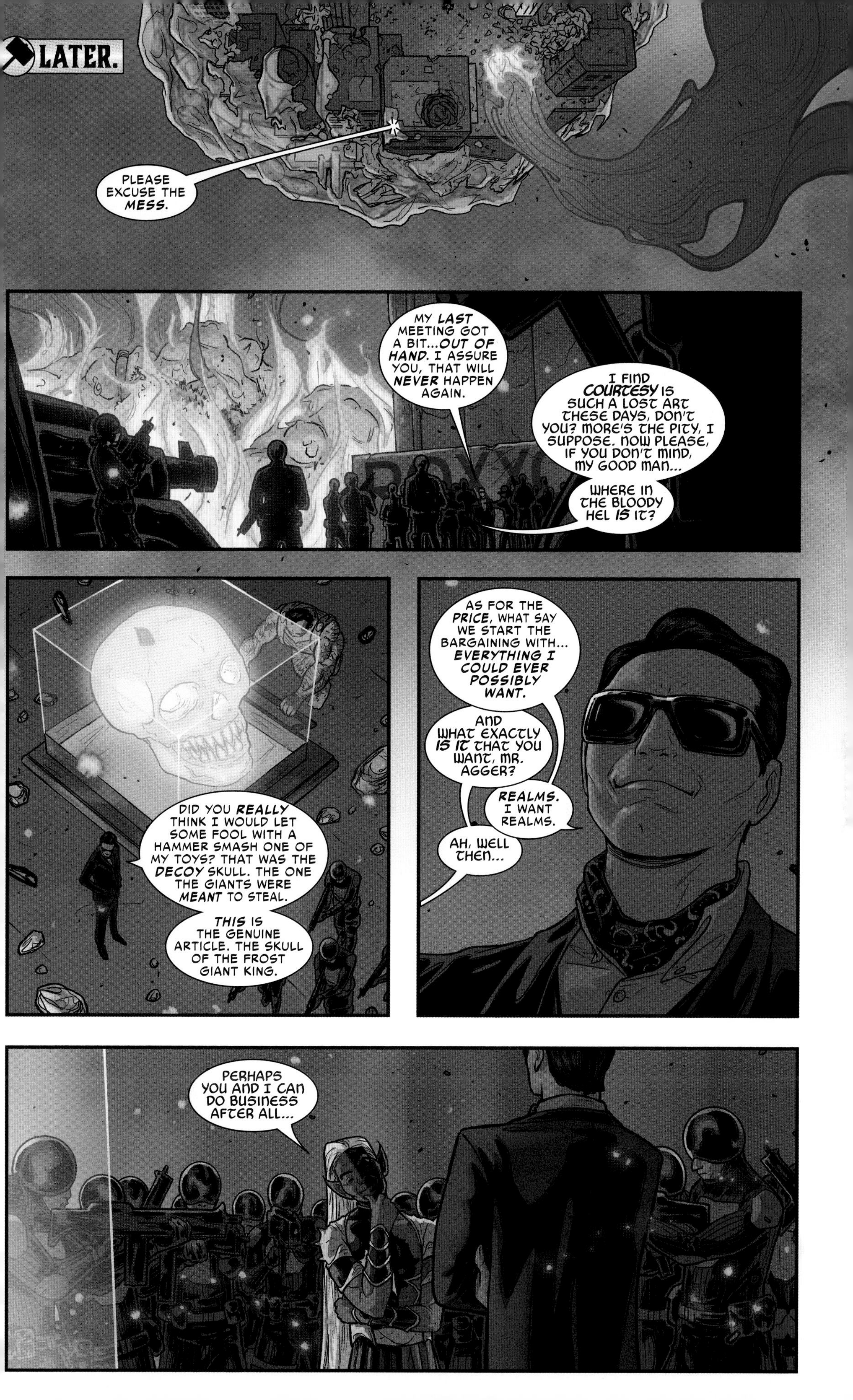
LATER.
PLEASE EXCUSE THE MESS.
MY LAST MEETING GOT A BIT...OUT OF HAND. I ASSURE YOU, THAT WILL NEVER HAPPEN AGAIN.
I FIND COURTESY IS SUCH A LOST ART THESE DAYS, DON'T YOU? MORE'S THE PITY, I SUPPOSE. NOW PLEASE, IF YOU DON'T MIND, MY GOOD MAN...
WHERE IN THE BLOODY HEL IS IT?
DID YOU REALLY THINK I WOULD LET SOME FOOL WITH A HAMMER SMASH ONE OF MY TOYS? THAT WAS THE DECOY SKULL. THE ONE THE GIANTS WERE MEANT TO STEAL.
THIS IS THE GENUINE ARTICLE. THE SKULL OF THE FROST GIANT KING.
AS FOR THE PRICE, WHAT SAY WE START THE BARGAINING WITH... EVERYTHING I COULD EVER POSSIBLY WANT.
AND WHAT EXACTLY IS IT THAT YOU WANT, MR. AGGER?
REALMS. I WANT REALMS.
AH, WELL THEN...
PERHAPS YOU AND I CAN DO BUSINESS AFTER ALL...

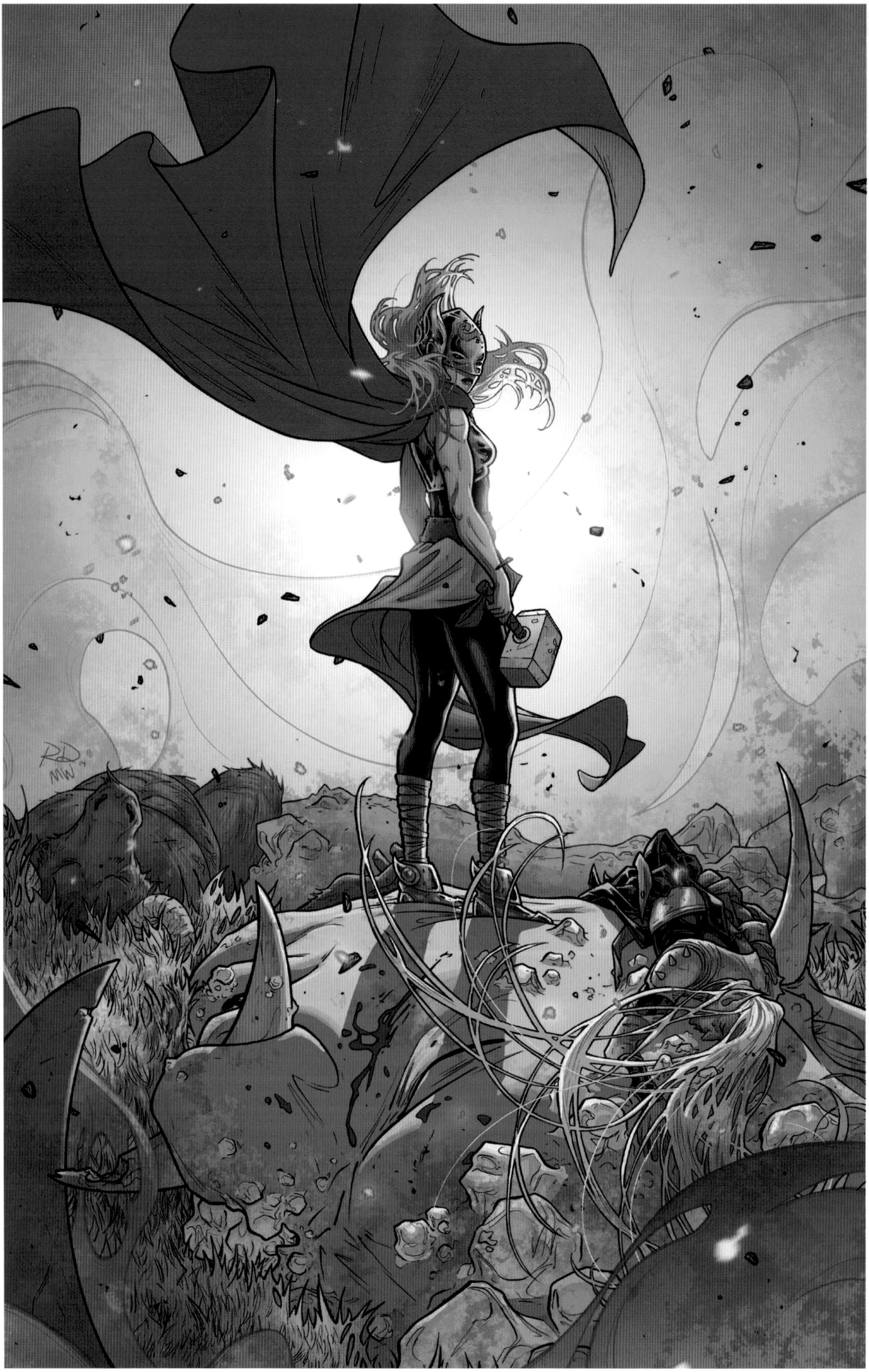

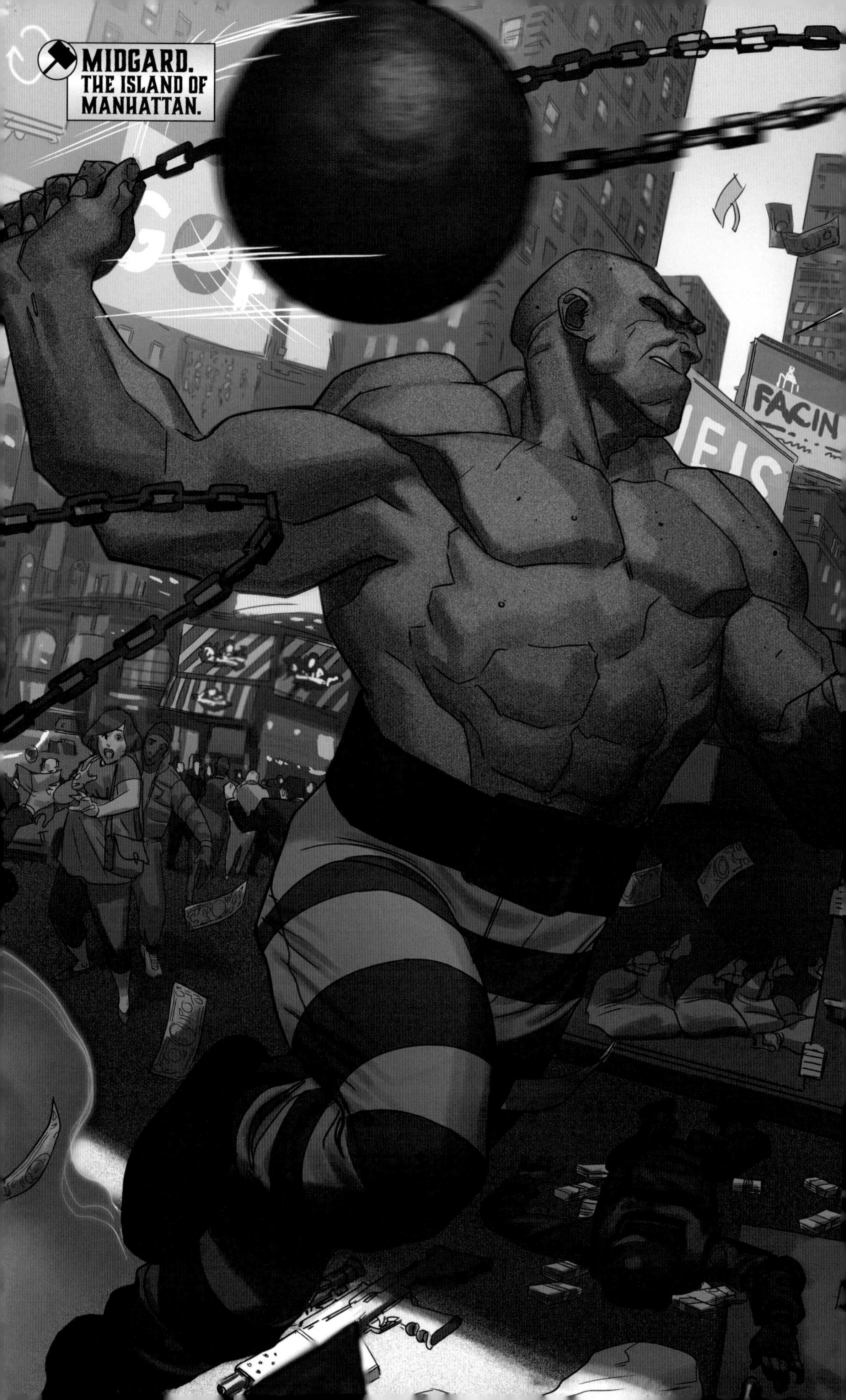
MIDGARD. THE ISLAND OF MANHATTAN.
FACIN

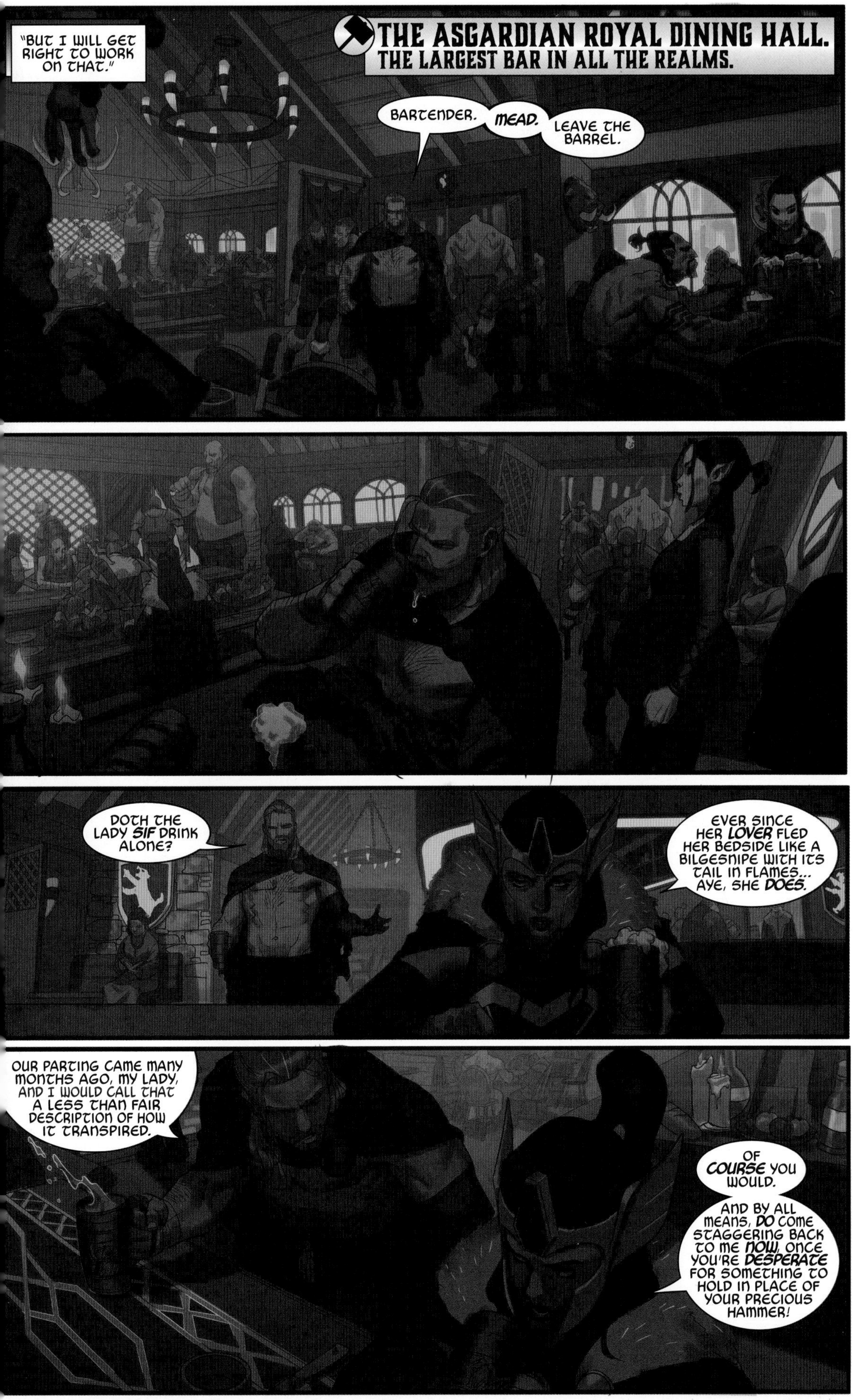
"BUT I WILL GET RIGHT TO WORK ON THAT."
THE ASGARDIAN ROYAL DINING HALL.
THE LARGEST BAR IN ALL THE REALMS.
BARTENDER. MEAD. LEAVE THE BARREL.
DOTH THE LADY SIF DRINK ALONE?
EVER SINCE HER LOVER FLED HER BEDSIDE LIKE A BILGESNIPE WITH ITS TAIL IN FLAMES... AYE, SHE DOES.
OUR PARTING CAME MANY MONTHS AGO, MY LADY, AND I WOULD CALL THAT A LESS THAN FAIR DESCRIPTION OF HOW IT TRANSPIRED.
OF COURSE YOU WOULD.
AND BY ALL MEANS, DO COME STAGGERING BACK TO ME NOW, ONCE YOU'RE DESPERATE FOR SOMETHING TO HOLD IN PLACE OF YOUR PRECIOUS HAMMER!

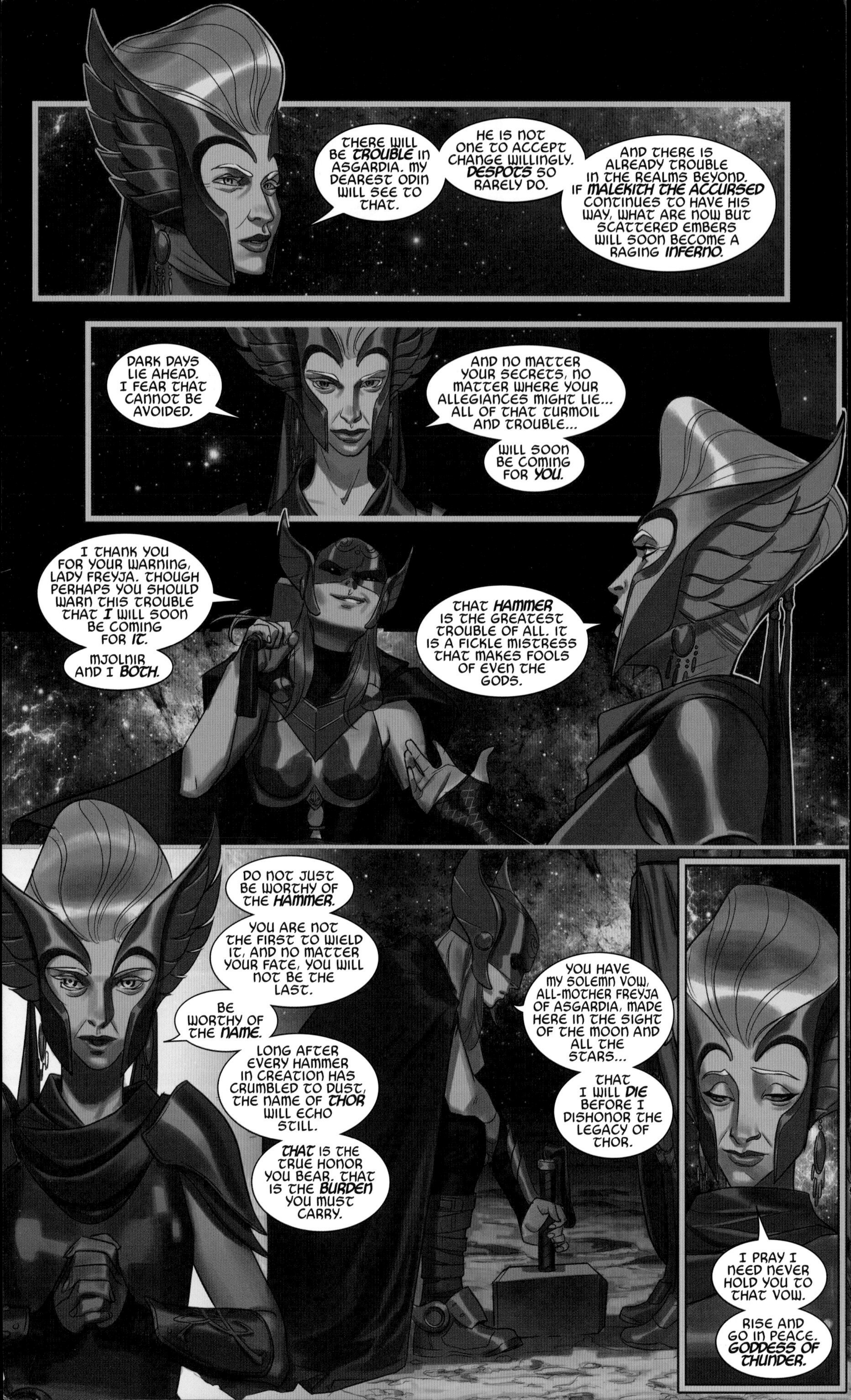
THERE WILL BE TROUBLE IN ASGARDIA. MY DEAREST ODIN WILL SEE TO THAT.
HE IS NOT ONE TO ACCEPT CHANGE WILLINGLY. DESPOTS SO RARELY DO.
AND THERE IS ALREADY TROUBLE IN THE REALMS BEYOND. IF MALEKITH THE ACCURSED CONTINUES TO HAVE HIS WAY, WHAT ARE NOW BUT SCATTERED EMBERS WILL SOON BECOME A RAGING INFERNO.
DARK DAYS LIE AHEAD. I FEAR THAT CANNOT BE AVOIDED.
AND NO MATTER YOUR SECRETS, NO MATTER WHERE YOUR ALLEGIANCES MIGHT LIE... ALL OF THAT TURMOIL AND TROUBLE...
WILL SOON BE COMING FOR YOU.
I THANK YOU FOR YOUR WARNING, LADY FREYJA. THOUGH PERHAPS YOU SHOULD WARN THIS TROUBLE THAT I WILL SOON BE COMING FOR IT.
MJOLNIR AND I BOTH.
THAT HAMMER IS THE GREATEST TROUBLE OF ALL. IT IS A FICKLE MISTRESS THAT MAKES FOOLS OF EVEN THE GODS.
DO NOT JUST BE WORTHY OF THE HAMMER.
YOU ARE NOT THE FIRST TO WIELD IT, AND NO MATTER YOUR FATE, YOU WILL NOT BE THE LAST.
BE WORTHY OF THE NAME.
LONG AFTER EVERY HAMMER IN CREATION HAS CRUMBLED TO DUST, THE NAME OF THOR WILL ECHO STILL.
THAT IS THE TRUE HONOR YOU BEAR. THAT IS THE BURDEN YOU MUST CARRY.
YOU HAVE MY SOLEMN VOW, ALL-MOTHER FREYJA OF ASGARDIA, MADE HERE IN THE SIGHT OF THE MOON AND ALL THE STARS...
THAT I WILL DIE BEFORE I DISHONOR THE LEGACY OF THOR.
I PRAY I NEED NEVER HOLD YOU TO THAT VOW.
RISE AND GO IN PEACE, GODDESS OF THUNDER.

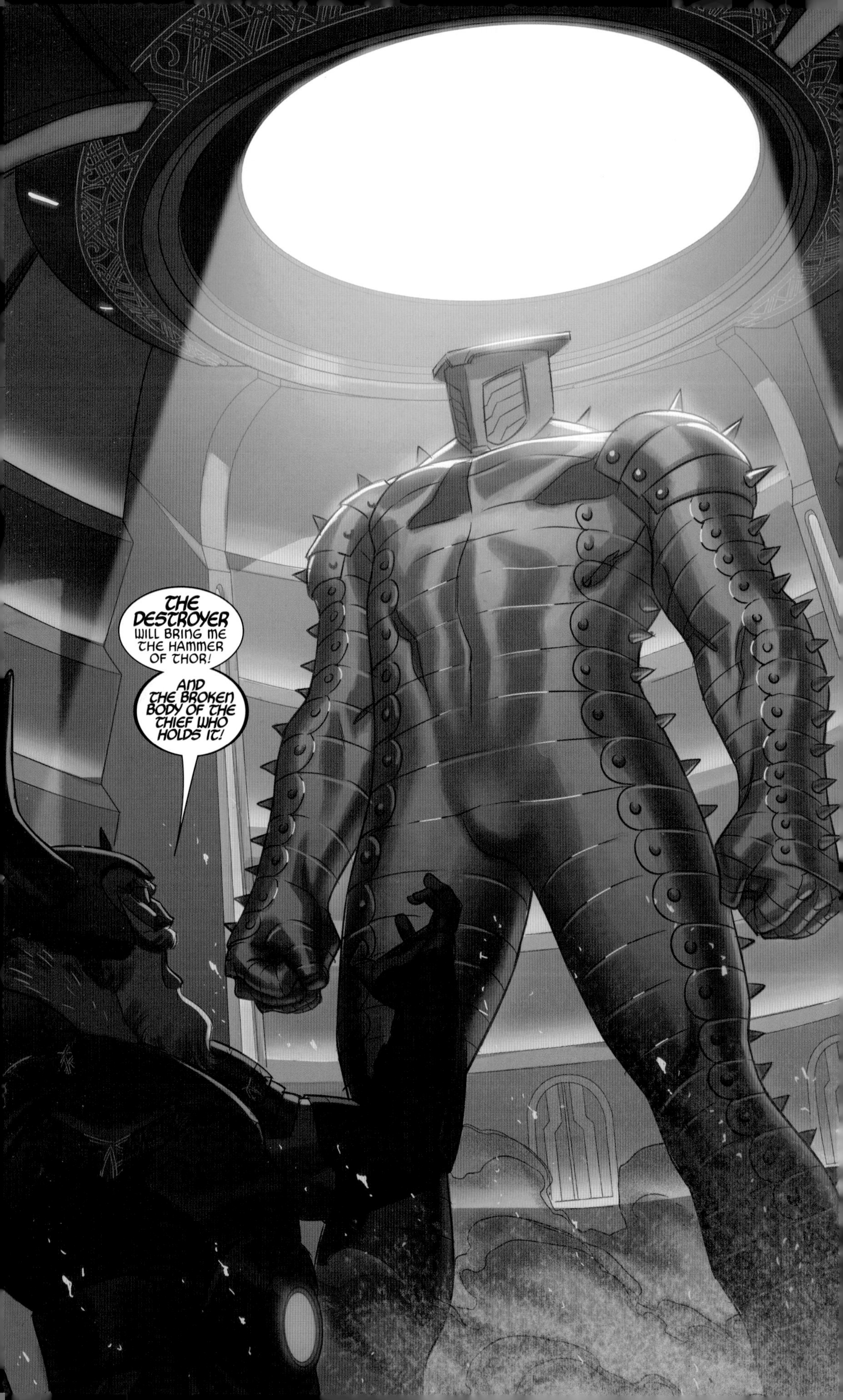
THE DESTROYER WILL BRING ME THE HAMMER OF THOR!
AND THE BROKEN BODY OF THE THIEF WHO HOLDS IT!

THOR

Variant Cover Gallery

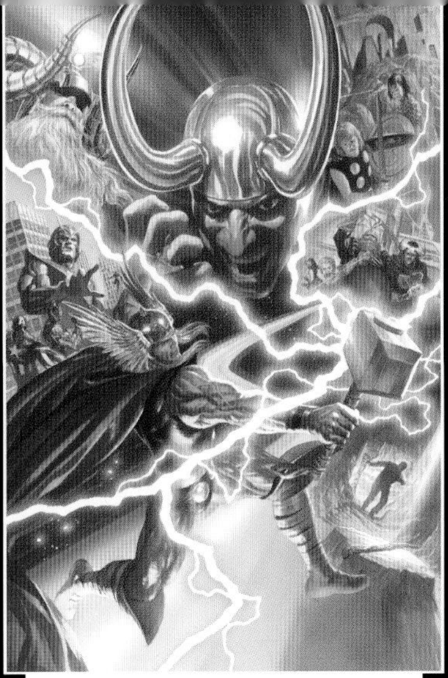

Thor #1 Marvel 75th Anniversary
Variant Cover By Alex Ross

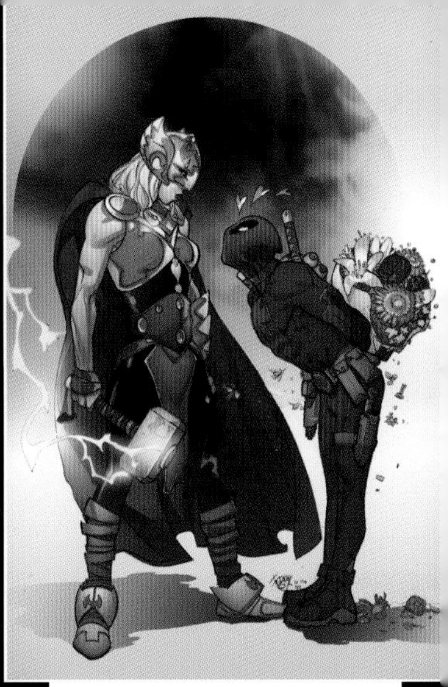

Thor #1 Variant Cover
By Pascual Ferry

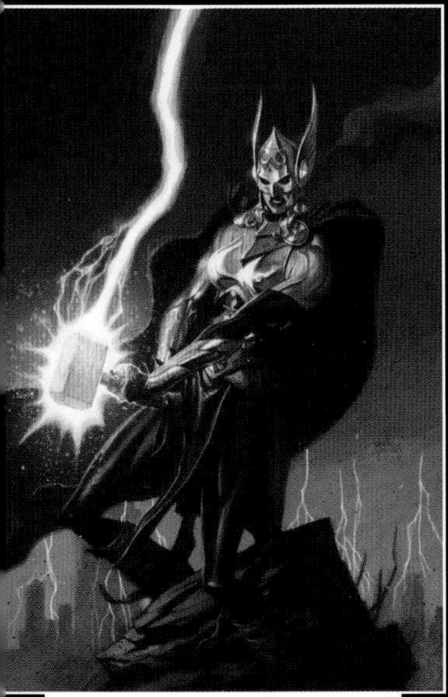

Thor #1 Variant Cover
By Milo Manara

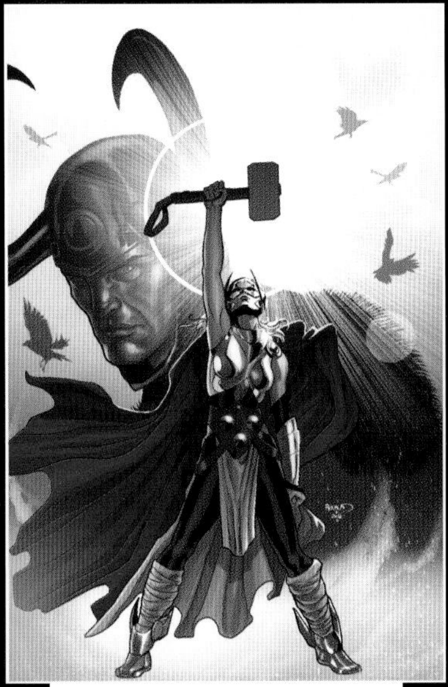

Thor #1 Variant Cover
By Paul Renaud

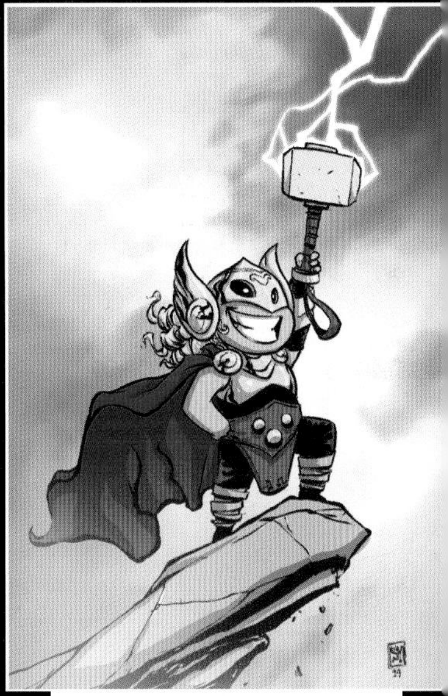

Thor #1 Variant Cover
By Skottie Young

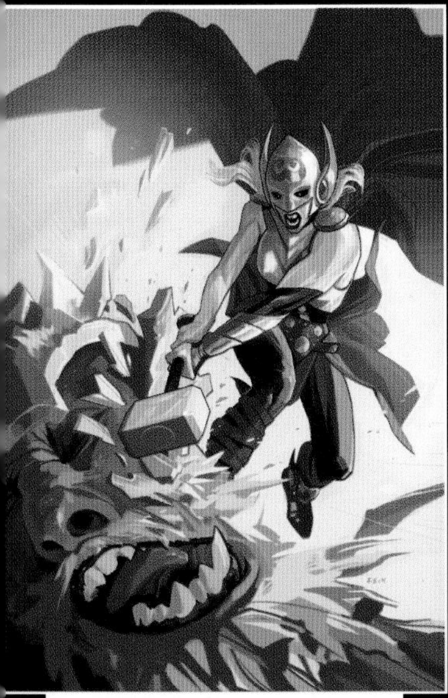

Thor #1 Variant Cover
By Fiona Staples

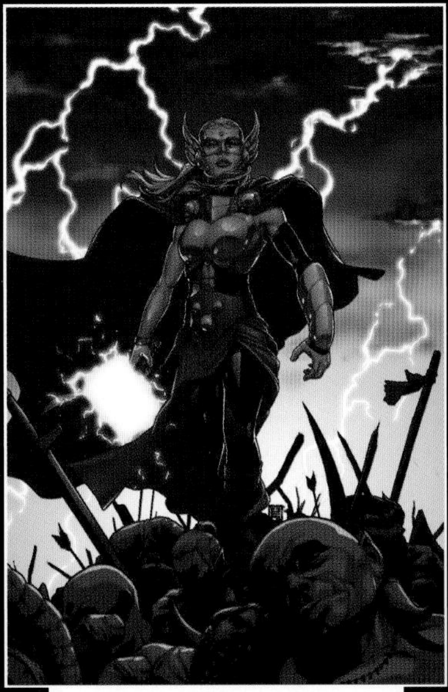

Thor #1 Variant Cover
By John Tyler Christopher

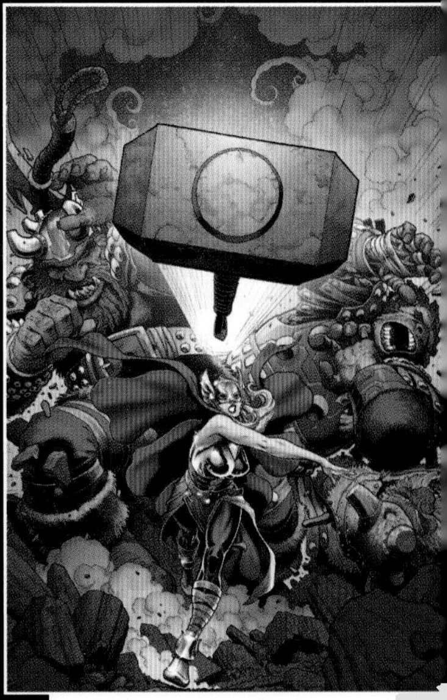

Thor #1 Variant Cover
By Art Adams

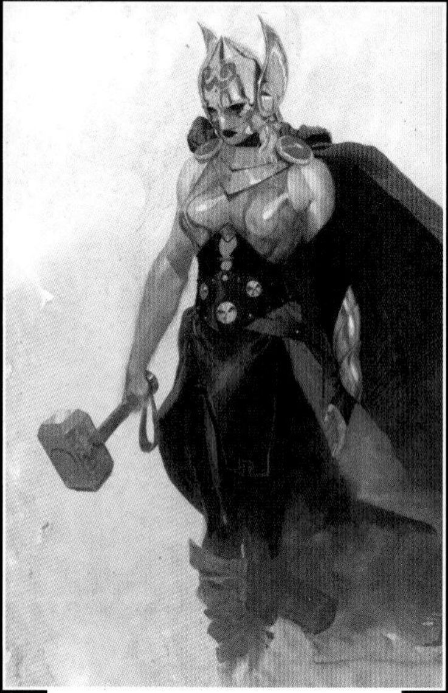

Thor #1 Variant Cover
By Esad Ribic

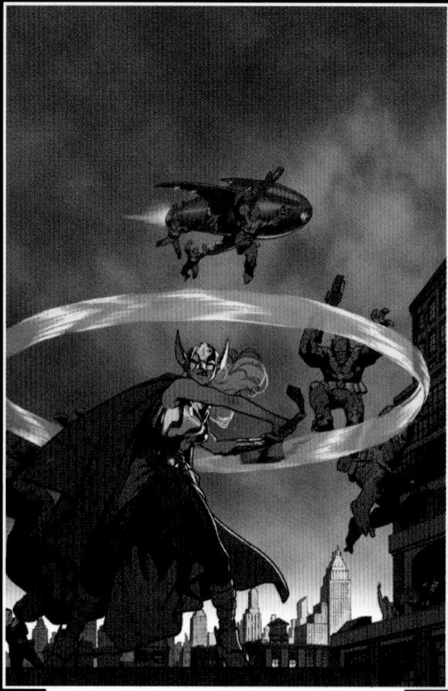

Thor #1 Variant Cover
By Jorge Molina

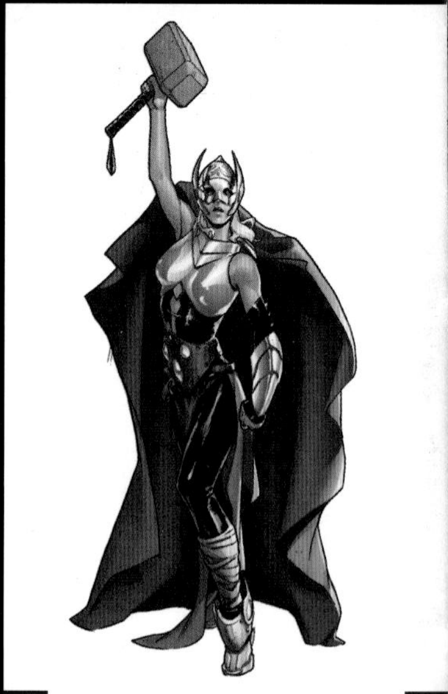

Thor #1 Variant Cover
By Sara Pichelli

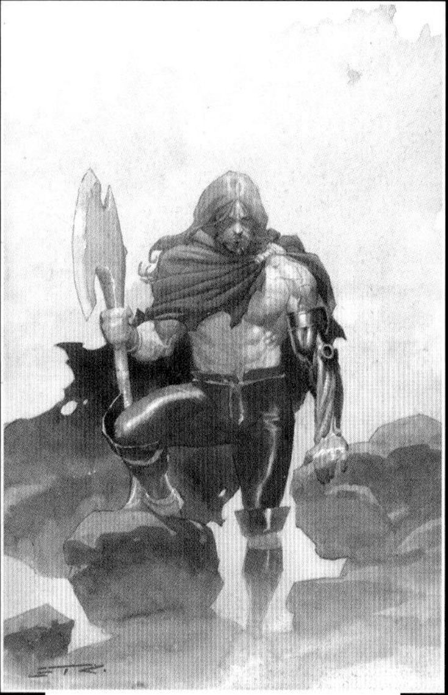

Thor #2 Variant Cover
By Esad Ribic

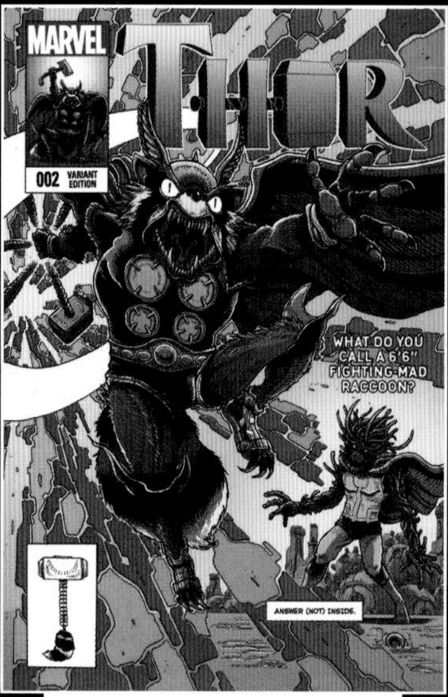
MARVEL
002 VARIANT EDITION
THOR
WHAT DO YOU CALL A 6'6" FIGHTING-MAD RACCOON?
ANSWER (NOT) INSIDE.

Thor #2 Variant Cover
By James Stokoe

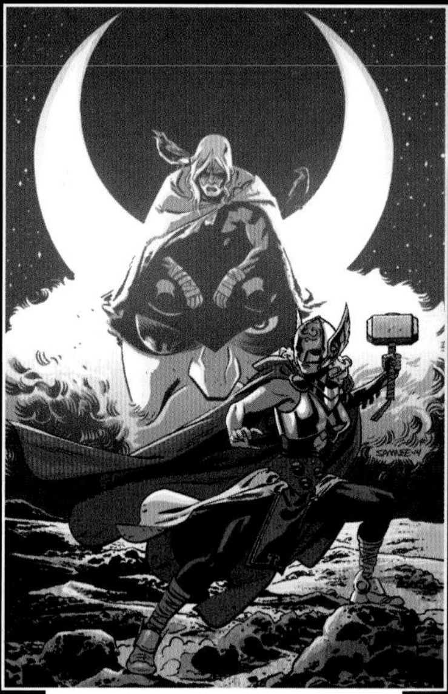

Thor #2 Variant Cover
By Chris Samnee

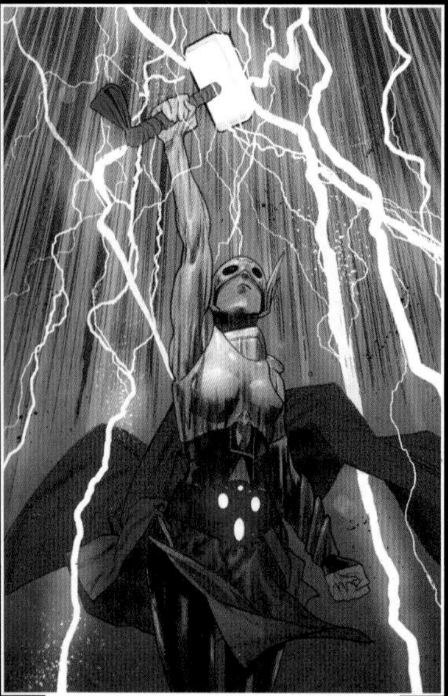

Thor #3 Variant Cover
By James Harren

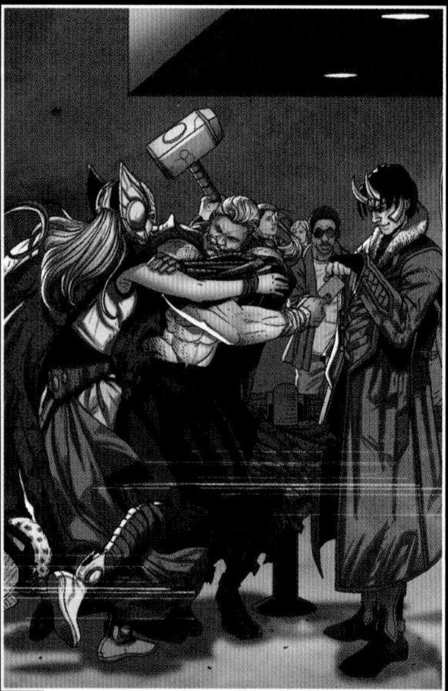

Thor #4 Variant Cover
By Salvador Larroca

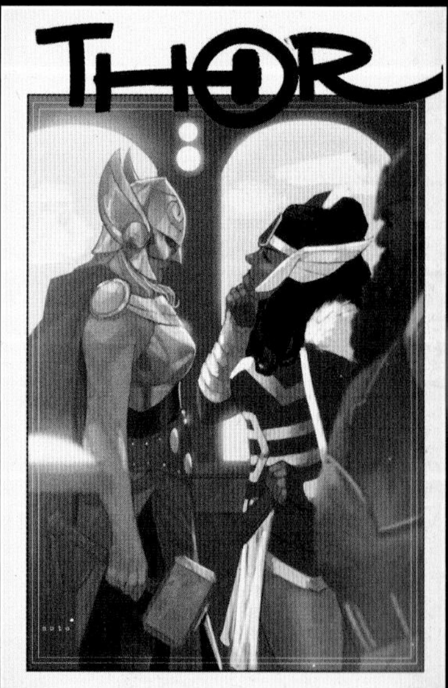
THOR

Thor #5 Variant Cover
By Phil Noto